ANTONY AND CLEOPATRA

ANTONY AND CLEOPATRA

William Shakespeare

Edited by
CEDRIC WATTS

WORDSWORTH CLASSICS

For my husband
ANTHONY JOHN RANSON
with love from your wife, the publisher.
Eternally grateful for your unconditional love.

Readers who are interested in other titles from
Wordsworth Editions are invited to visit our website at
www.wordsworth-editions.com

First published in 2000 by Wordsworth Editions Ltd.,
8B East Street, Ware, Hertfordshire SG12 9HJ.
A revised edition appeared in 2004.
This new edition, with newly-edited text and
apparatus, appeared in 2006.

ISBN 978 1 85326 075 9

Wordsworth Editions
is the company founded in 1987 by
MICHAEL TRAYLER

Typeset in Great Britain by Antony Gray
Printed and bound in Great Britain by Clays Ltd, Elcograf S.p.A.

CONTENTS

GENERAL INTRODUCTION

In the new Wordsworth Classics' Shakespeare Series, the inaugural volumes, *Romeo and Juliet*, *The Merchant of Venice* and *Henry V*, have been followed by *The Taming of the Shrew*, *A Midsummer Night's Dream*, *Much Ado about Nothing*, *Julius Cæsar*, *Hamlet*, *Twelfth Night*, *Measure for Measure*, *Othello*, *Macbeth*, *King Lear*, *Antony and Cleopatra*, *The Winter's Tale* and *The Tempest*. Previously, the Wordsworth Shakespeare volumes often adopted, by arrangement, an earlier Cambridge University Press text. The new series, however, consists of fresh editions specially commissioned for Wordsworth Classics. Each play in this emergent Shakespeare Series is accompanied by a standard apparatus, including an introduction, explanatory notes and a glossary. The textual editing takes account of recent scholarship, while giving the material a careful reappraisal. The apparatus is, however, concise rather than elaborate. We hope that the resultant volumes prove to be handy, reliable and helpful. Above all, we hope that, from Shakespeare's works, readers will derive pleasure, wisdom, provocations, challenges, and insights: insights into his culture and ours, and into the era of civilisation to which his writings have made (and continue to make) such potently influential contributions. Shakespeare's eloquence will, undoubtedly, re-echo 'in states unborn and accents yet unknown'.

CEDRIC WATTS
Series Editor

INTRODUCTION

Eleven of Shakespeare's works are customarily classified as tragedies; and, of these, *Antony and Cleopatra* is one of the very greatest. It is a drama of love, history, morality and politics; and its combinations of striking incidents, complex characterisations and exuberant eloquence have guaranteed its long cultural life since its first appearance around 1607, and seem likely to guarantee a further life of many years to come. For present-day audiences, it offers a timely demonstration of the interlinkages of power, affluence, lust, corruption and decadence.

Most of the historical material for the play was supplied by 'The Life of Marcus Antonius' in *The Lives of the Noble Grecians and Romanes* (1579), Sir Thomas North's translation into English of Jacques Amyot's French translation of a work in Greek (dated approximately 100 A.D.) by Plutarch. The original was a mixture of fact, legend and fiction. It became further modified in course of translation; and Shakespeare added many new embellishments. For instance, North's Plutarch had dealt relatively curtly with the death of Fulvia, Antony's militant wife:

> But by good fortune, his wife Fulvia going to meet with Antonius, sickened by the way, and died in the city of Sicyone: and therefore Octavius Cæsar and he were the easilier made friends together.[1]

In the play, in contrast, Fulvia's death receives detailed commentary by Antony and Enobarbus: a commentary variously melancholy, philosophical and bawdily cynical. The effect is to render rather more sympathetic the characterisation of Antony and to expose some misogyny within Enobarbus's military camaraderie and 'male bonding'.

Plutarch's account of Antony's life is lengthy and sometimes digressive. (One digression is the story of Timon of Athens, which provided the basis of a peculiarly different drama.) Shakespeare, as is customary when he adapts chronicles, has clarified the narrative by his selection of material and has compressed the time-scale to increase dramatic momentum. Reports of Antony's lengthy campaigns are greatly reduced; 'human interest' is variously enhanced; and incidents of comedy are magnified or introduced. In Plutarch, Antony's marriage to Octavia lasts long enough for her to raise children whom he has fathered (and he then evicts them all from their house in Rome). In Shakespeare, the marital relationship seems to last no longer than a few weeks. Some episodes presenting Antony and Cleopatra in a particularly harsh light are absent from the play. Plutarch says that when Antony's army suffered a defeat at the hands of the Medes, Antony punished his men by sentencing one-tenth of them to death: literally, a decimation. Again, Plutarch explains that Cleopatra, seeking painless ways to die, arranged tests in which numerous men were obliged to take poison or be stung by snakes. She looked on (anticipating the practices of Nazi extermination-camp doctors) as the victims of her experiments perished, some 'with grievous torments'. While eschewing such material, Shakespeare has greatly expanded the depiction of the festivities on Pompey's galley, so that we see the great dictators of the ancient world turning into the besotted subjects of alcohol. Even the imperious Octavius cannot master his own tongue, for it 'spleets' (slurs or confuses) its utterance; and the warlords are all 'anticked', buffoonish. Irony thus plays upon and around so many of the play's incidents and affirmations, while mighty rhetoric is repeatedly displayed and questioned.

When Shakespeare converts Plutarch's prose narrative into dramatic poetry, there is usually (as commentators often note) an immense gain in sensuous richness and vitality, and a subtle thematic co-ordination emerges. One frequently-employed illustration is the description of Cleopatra's voyage down the river Cydnus to impress and woo Mark Antony. Plutarch's description begins thus:

[S]he disdained to set forth otherwise, but to take her barge in the river of Cydnus, the poop whereof was of gold, the sails of purple, and the oars of silver, which kept stroke in rowing after the sound of the music of flutes, howboys, citherns, viols, and such other instruments as they played upon in the barge. And now for the person of herself: she was laid under a pavilion of cloth of gold of tissue, apparelled and attired like the goddess Venus, commonly drawn in picture: and hard by her, on either hand of her, pretty fair boys apparelled as painters do set forth god Cupid, with little fans in their hands, with the which they fanned wind upon her.[2]

In the play, in Act 2, scene 2, Enobarbus says this:

> The barge she sat in, like a burnished throne,
> Burnt on the water: the poop was beaten gold;
> Purple the sails, and so perfumèd that
> The winds were love-sick with them; the oars were silver,
> Which to the tune of flutes kept stroke, and made
> The water which they beat to follow faster,
> As amorous of their strokes. For her own person,
> It beggared all description. She did lie,
> In her pavilion, cloth-of-gold, of tissue,
> O'er-picturing that Venus where we see
> The fancy out-work nature. On each side her
> Stood pretty dimpled boys, like smiling Cupids,
> With divers-coloured fans, whose wind did seem
> To glow the delicate cheeks which they did cool,
> And what they undid did.

You can see at once the difference between the relatively inert catalogue of details offered by Plutarch and the relatively animated description offered by Enobarbus. Of course, matters are complicated by the fact that Shakespeare's speaker is no historian but a soldier speaking to fellow-soldiers. Naturally, he'll be inclined to exaggerate the great experiences of his travels: from ancient times to the present, that has been the case when soldier yarns to soldier. We know that Enobarbus elsewhere is one of the shrewdest critics of Cleopatra. But his account also conveys a truth within the exaggeration: Cleopatra, like some Hollywood star and director, has a talent for glamorous stage-management. She is obviously seeking to impress, but she can succeed gloriously in doing so.

Plutarch says that she determined 'to take her barge' (her sumptuous vessel of state) 'in the river of Cydnus'; Enobarbus, on the other hand, claims that her barge, 'like a burnished throne, / Burnt on the water'. 'Burnt' is a hyperbolic way of saying 'Shone brightly', but it does suggest an actively blazing quality: amid water, there is fire. (Already there's an anticipation of her death-scene: 'I am fire and air; my other elements / I give to baser life'.) In Plutarch, the poop was gold; in Enobarbus's speech, it has become 'beaten gold' (hammered into sheets), partly because the word 'beaten' has alliterative richness, echoing several consonants of 'barge', 'burnished', and 'Burnt'. The sound-patterning and the rhythm of iambic pentameter provide the orally-voluptuous sound-track to accompany the exotic motion-picture. In Plutarch, the sails are 'of purple'; in Enobarbus's account, they are not only purple but so richly perfumed that '[t]he winds were love-sick with them', so that the vessel seems eroticised: a dynamic centre of desire, it seduces nature itself. Plutarch said that the oars kept time to music; Enobarbus adds the detail that the beating of the oars 'made / The water which they beat to follow faster, / As amorous of their strokes', so that, again, while the poetic rhythm enhances the evoked action, the vessel seems seductive, and nature seems voluptuously anthropomorphic. What Enobarbus adds to the description of Cleopatra herself is the sense of her transcendent excess: she indeed beggars description. Plutarch said that she looked like Venus 'commonly drawn in picture'; but Enobarbus offers a double hyperbole: if you see a picture of Venus in which the artist's imagination offers a better creation than does nature, know that Cleopatra in her own person surpasses that masterwork. Finally, in Plutarch, the cupidous boys merely 'fanned wind upon her'. According to Enobarbus, the fans are many-hued; and, more importantly, their draughts

did seem
To glow the delicate cheeks which they did cool,
And what they undid did.

It's a wonderfully evocative detail: delicate cheeks glowing as if heated rather than cooled; and that paradox, that the boys seem to be restoring what they remove, frustrating their own endeavour, gains thematic resonance. Quite often in this play, endeavours will prove counter-productive and efforts may be self-defeating. For instance: the political marriage to Octavia fails to secure the desired 'perpetual amity'; in battle, Antony fights renegade followers, and thus seems 'to spend his fury / Upon himself'; then he botches his suicide; and Octavius's wiles are thwarted by Cleopatra. At other times, actions may be seen as part of a process of cyclical renewal. The Nile's floods generate harvests. Cleopatra will be depicted as a cornucopian sexual paragon who ever supplies but never cloys: constantly gratifying but never sating, 'she makes hungry / Where most she satisfies'. And Antony's bounty, she claims, was an autumn which 'grew the more by reaping'. Finally, she 'is again for Cydnus, to meet Mark Antony'.

When you look back on Enobarbus's description, you see how it creates the impression that Cleopatra may be a second Venus, a goddess of love with power to animate seductively the vessel and its setting. The spectacle is showmanship, but, as described, it partakes of magic or miracle. The recollection by Enobarbus is itself showmanship too, if of a secondary order, but the responses by Agrippa ('O rare for Antony!', 'Rare Egyptian!' and 'Royal wench!') confirm its success. And the larger context is typically ironic. This is the meeting in Rome at which Antony, widower of Fulvia, readily agrees to marry Octavia (Octavius Cæsar's sister) to cement a political alliance. Here he betrays Cleopatra, to whom he had sworn fidelity; and soon he'll betray Octavia, in spite of promising her that he will henceforth be honourable.

When reporting the manner of Cleopatra's eventual death, Plutarch says that a countryman brought her some figs, that possibly an 'aspic' (snake) was concealed among them, and that if she was bitten by it, she was bitten in the arm. Shakespeare develops the character of this countryman so that he becomes a shrewd fellow with a predictable taste for bawdy innuendoes. When Cleopatra asks him if he recalls any people who have been killed by the biting of the snake (the 'pretty worm of Nilus'), he replies:

Very many, men, and women too. I heard of one of them no longer than yesterday: a very honest woman, but something given to lie, as a woman should not do but in the way of honesty; how she died of the biting of it, what pain she felt. Truly, she makes a very good report o'th'worm . . .

The agent of death is jocularly confused with the agent of life. Serpent and phallus, suffering and sexual desire are knowingly intermingled. The ambiguity of the words 'lie' and 'died' invokes the notion of a woman's sexual intercourse and orgasm. So, even as she prepares her suicide, Cleopatra is given a mocking reminder of the sensual pleasures which have constituted so central a part of her life. (She herself had been called by Antony the 'serpent of old Nile'.) Indeed, as Iras dies, Cleopatra maintains the imagery of an erotic death:

> If thou and nature can so gently part,
> The stroke of death is as a lover's pinch,
> Which hurts, and is desired.

In Plutarch, the asp is applied only to an arm. In Shakespeare, Cleopatra first applies an asp to her breast. And, in a striking conceit, she says:

> Peace, peace:
> Dost thou not see my baby at my breast,
> That sucks the nurse asleep?

In this startling juxtaposition which is both poignant and perverse, the image of a woman being poisoned to death by a serpent is fused with the image of Cleopatra as mother, breastfeeding a baby. The detail may, perhaps subliminally, remind us of Octavius's warning to Cleopatra that if she eluded him by suicide, he would execute her children. So her image of the loving mother is evoked by a woman who is abandoning her real offspring to their fate.[3] But our attention is focused predominantly on the spectacular majesty of Cleopatra's death. Clearly, true to her character, she has stage-managed it as impressive spectacle:

> Give me my robe, put on my crown: I have
> Immortal longings in me.

The staging is regal, and the eloquence is unsurpassed: she is arrogant, vain, jealous, reflective, poignant; she evokes for us the image of an afterlife in which she may indeed walk proudly with Antony. After her vacillations and duplicities, her tricks and changes, she does indeed, at last, prove 'marble-constant'; by her courage, she can claim him as husband. What Charmian says, by way of epitaph, seems totally apt:

> Now boast thee, Death, in thy possession lies
> A lass unparalleled.

Equally apt is the subsequent detail. After saying

> And golden Phœbus never be beheld
> Of eyes so royal[,]

Charmian adds:

> > Your crown's awry:
> I'll mend it, and then play.

The human touch: in this spectacular death-performance, there's a flaw, a touch of human fallibility and even absurdity: a crown awry, lopsided.

As we noted, Enobarbus had declared: 'Age cannot wither her, nor custom stale / Her infinite variety.' So Shakespeare, as dramatist, was setting himself a peculiarly difficult task: to present a female character proclaimed immensely complex. The result was the fullest female characterisation in the whole of the drama of the Elizabethan and Jacobean periods; a characterisation arguably still unsurpassed as a creation for the theatre. According to Plutarch, Cleopatra was 38 when she died, having reigned for 22 years.[4] As portrayed by Shakespeare, she is voluptuously beautiful, experienced in love and politics, seductive, sensual, passionate, crafty, jealous, vindictive, cowardly, brave, false, true, generous, mean, petty and changeable, but finally, as we have seen, mortally loyal to Antony. Morally, Octavia is, no doubt, superior to Cleopatra; but, if you use the criterion not of moral virtue but of fulness of being, Cleopatra wins. The more we say, 'This part of Cleopatra seems good, this part seems bad', the more we test this aspect and that, the more the scales of judgement tend to collapse under the sheer weight of qualities that we're putting into the opposed pans of the moral balance. The play seems to ask repeatedly, 'Which is better, a virtuous self or a full self? Should people be good or should they be vital? Can rational prudence match tragic intensity?'.

From the very opening of the play, such questioning is established as a co-ordinator of the structure. In the first speech, Philo, the veteran campaigner, declares that though Antony was once a general as impressive as the god Mars himself, he has become 'the bellows and the fan / To cool a gypsy's lust': what can be observed now is

> The triple pillar of the world transformed
> Into a strumpet's fool.

Yet immediately, as Antony and Cleopatra themselves enter, a contrast is declared. Philo had talked hyperbolically of the warlord that Antony had been, and contemptuously of his enslavement by sexual lust; but Antony now talks of his love for Cleopatra in hyperbolically romantic terms – 'There's beggary in the love that can be reckoned'. What Philo called a foolish infatuation, Antony depicts as a transcendent passion which cannot be measured by earthly standards. Philo thinks he has summed it up; Antony says it can't be summed up. Philo had lamented the reduction of the triple pillar of the world; Antony says that the known world and heaven itself won't suffice to define his love. Then, at the very moment when he's stressing transcendence, there enters the messenger bearing reminders of this world's demands and practicalities: 'News, my good lord, from Rome'; to which Antony replies curtly, 'Grates me: the sum' (i.e., 'That grates. Give me the gist!'). We are being tugged by quite contrasting judgements and even quite contrasting modes of speech. There are oscillations in the diction as well as in the claims.

These oscillations are also visual. At the beginning we see a campaigner telling an acquaintance that Cleopatra is a mere brown gypsy and a whore, but then Cleopatra herself enters with Antony and her ladies, 'with eunuchs fanning her': a whole procession. On stage it's usually a spectacular entry, displaying majesty, opulence, colour, beauty, the exotically 'oriental' and the decadently luxurious. Visually, then, a stern moral judgement is brought into collision with a largely aesthetic judgement, and the claims of war and politics collide with the claims of sexual passion. And just as we adapt to the new perspective, in comes that messenger to say (in effect): love orates but business calls.

The sense of this play's remarkable richness derives largely from the ways in which action, imagery and spectacle establish patterns of mutually-reinforcing contrasts: warfare contrasting with festivity, luxury competing against hardihood, the lofty against the mundane, the vast against the petty, sweet against sour, stillness against motion, the majestic against the sceptically realistic, the imaginative against the practical, the eternal against the temporal. The play makes our judgements veer repeatedly, and the questions it poses lead us not to simple answers but to apprehension of the prodigal complexity of the whole dramatised wrangle. This is (so to speak) a drama of 'to-and-fro-ness', whether in location, in plot, in characterisation or in imagery. The location shifts repeatedly between Alexandria and Rome, with excursions to Sicily, Misena, Athens, Actium and elsewhere. In the plot, political fortunes change rapidly. One day, Lepidus is a triumvir; the next, he's a captive. One day, Pompey holds the lives of Antony and Octavius in his hand; another day, he has been killed. In the battles between Octavius and Antony, fortune first favours Octavius, then it favours Antony; and finally Octavius prevails. Antony's own allegiances veer wildly: he's capable of swearing his love to Cleopatra and yet of marrying Octavia; then he'll return to Cleopatra, but will later revile and denounce her as a 'kite', a 'boggler' and a 'triple-turned whore', while Octavia is 'a gem of women'. Cleopatra can be seen as both a strumpet and 'Egypt' (country personified), as an incarnation of Isis and Venus, and even as the 'day o'th'world'. Antony is 'painted one way like a Gorgon' but 'the other way's a Mars'; he's associated with Hercules and Bacchus; yet he's also the callous bully who has a messenger ruthlessly flogged. He's the war-lord who has stoically suffered privation, even drinking 'the gilded puddle / Which beasts would cough at', yet he's also the foolish deserter who, at the height of a battle, lets down his side by fleeing after Cleopatra. When she proclaims him one who 'bestrid the ocean', speaking like 'rattling thunder' and scattering 'realms and islands' like coins from his pocket, she pauses to say to Dolabella,

> Think you there was, or might be, such a man
> As this I dreamt of?

And Dolabella replies: 'Gentle madam, no.'

In the imagery, there's a pervasive theme of mobility, oscillation and elemental interchange. Cæsar says:

> This common body,
> Like to a vagabond flag upon the stream,

> Goes to and back, lackeying the varying tide,
> To rot itself with motion.

He means that the common people are fickle in their loyalties; but the tidal imagery flows beyond its immediate occasion, and steeps more of the play than it first seems to do. We see the ebb and flow of 'the varying tide' in the relationships between the central characters and their political fortunes: Cæsar and Antony opposed, then in alliance, then opposed; Antony and Cleopatra in alliance, next at odds, then in alliance, and finally in defeat. Though Octavius speaks contemptuously of the lovers' relationship, it is he who provides their flattering epitaph:

> No grave upon the earth shall clip in it
> A pair so famous.

When we look back, we can see that throughout the play, Shakespeare has set a variety of orthodox ethical tests around the central figures. There's the test of virtuous sexual conduct. By that test, Octavia wins and Antony and Cleopatra lose. There's the test of political and military judgement. By that test, Octavius wins. There's the test of practical self-preserving common sense. There Dercetus wins, and Antony and Cleopatra lose again. Then there's that test of powerful people which Shakespeare was particularly fond of applying: the test of magnanimity and generosity to social inferiors. Here there's a mixed answer. Cleopatra is both friendly and familiar with some servants and a bully to others. Antony can be hearty and companionable to his men, but he can also let them down. He's sufficiently generous to send Enobarbus's belongings to their owner when Enobarbus defects, but he can be brutal to a messenger. Enobarbus himself, veering between admiration and scorn, loyalty to and defection from his master, eulogy and mockery of Cleopatra, typifies the play's strategy.

Octavius claims that Antony is being 'unmanned', demeaned, made effeminate, by his love for Cleopatra. He says of Antony:

> [H]e fishes, drinks, and wastes
> The lamps of night in revel; is not more manlike
> Than Cleopatra, nor the Queen of Ptolemy
> More womanly than he . . .

That's part of his severe moral indictment. But, later, Cleopatra gives her own account of fishing expeditions and revelry:

> My music playing far off, I will betray
> Tawny-finned fishes; my bended hook shall pierce
> Their slimy jaws, and, as I draw them up,
> I'll think them every one an Antony,
> And say 'Ah ha; y'are caught.'

Charmian then recalls the time that Cleopatra had fooled Antony by arranging for a diver to fix a salt-water fish to his hook; and Cleopatra responds:

> That time – O times! –
> I laughed him out of patience; and that night
> I laughed him into patience; and next morn,
> Ere the ninth hour, I drunk him to his bed;
> Then put my tires and mantles on him, whilst
> I wore his sword Philippan.

Octavius would regard her reflections as confirmation of his indictment of Antony as a dissolute hedonist, symbolically feminised. But Cleopatra's words convey with intimate credibility the vitality of this intensely spirited, sexual, pleasure-seeking and excess-invoking relationship with Antony.

  Thus, as we seek answers to the moral questions that the play raises, we increasingly recognise that standard criteria are being called into question by the irreducible intensity of the relationship of the 'mutual pair'. Ontology thus fights morality: the vital challenges the virtuous. Recurrently, the play's rhetoric expresses a fierce questing for definition. Antony and Cleopatra try to define themselves and each other by references to all the elements, to tides and dolphins, to seasons and fires, to kingdoms and empires, to sun, moon and stars. No comparison quite fits; no brief quotable definition sums up Antony and Cleopatra; some irony always saps the hyperboles; but that ransacking for definition, the constant quest – *that* gets defined abundantly in the play. Those two characters, those existential megalomaniacs, defiantly shout aloud what many people silently recognise: each of us can imagine a plenitude of personal selfhood that actual existence seldom seems to grant.

In *Antony and Cleopatra*, Shakespeare made superbly critical theatre about superbly theatrical lovers. No other play conveys with such an amplitude of eloquence, with such an eruption of world-ransacking images, the appeal, the variability and the dangers of a relationship which is at once intensely sexual and intensely political, and strives to go yet further. Here the imperialism of passion is both defined and opposed by the imperialism of martial domination. Defeated in the realm of political battles, Antony and Cleopatra triumph in the rhetorical realm of imagined (and imaginative) transcendent mutuality. There, they 'stand up peerless'.

Nevertheless, if you happen to be a messenger, don't go near them.

NOTES TO THE INTRODUCTION

1 Plutarch: *The Lives of the Noble Grecians and Romanes*, translated by Sir Thomas North (London: T. Vautroullier and J. Wight, 1579), p. 984. When quoting Plutarch, I modernise the spelling and punctuation.

2 Plutarch, p. 981.

3 In the event, Octavius killed Cæsarion, who represented a political threat, for he was supposed to be the son of Julius Cæsar. (Octavius was only Julius Cæsar's adopted son, being originally his great-nephew.) In contrast, Cleopatra's children by Antony survived. It is reported that Octavia raised them alongside her own children.

4 Plutarch, p. 1,010. Plutarch says that at the time of his death, Antony was either 53 or 56. Recent estimates are that Antony was then about 51, Cleopatra 38 or 39.

FURTHER READING
(in chronological order)

A. C. Bradley: *Oxford Lectures on Poetry*. London: Macmillan, 1909.

G. Wilson Knight: *The Imperial Theme*. London: Oxford University Press, 1931; revised edn.: London: Methuen, 1965.

Derek Traversi: *Shakespeare: The Roman Plays*. London: Hollis & Carter, 1963.

Ernest Schanzer: *The Problem Plays of Shakespeare: A Study of Julius Cæsar', 'Measure for Measure', 'Antony and Cleopatra'*. London: Routledge & Kegan Paul, 1963.

Narrative and Dramatic Sources of Shakespeare: Vol. V: The Roman Plays, ed. Geoffrey Bullough. London: Routledge & Kegan Paul, 1964.

Shakespeare: 'Antony and Cleopatra': A Casebook, ed. John Russell Brown. Basingstoke: Macmillan, 1968; revised edn., 1988; rpt., 1994.

Robin Lee: *Shakespeare: Antony and Cleopatra*. London: Arnold, 1971.

Twentieth Century Interpretations of 'Antony and Cleopatra', ed. Mark Rose. Englewood Cliffs, N. J.: Prentice-Hall, 1977.

Margaret Lamb: *'Antony and Cleopatra' on the English Stage*. Cranbury, N. J.: Associated University Presses, 1980.

Robert S. Miola: *Shakespeare's Rome*. Cambridge: Cambridge University Press, 1983.

Vivian Thomas: *Shakespeare's Roman Worlds*. London: Routledge, 1989.

M. M. Mahood: *Bit Parts in Shakespeare's Plays*. Cambridge: Cambridge University Press, 1992.

Mary Hamer: *Signs of Cleopatra: History, Politics, Representation*. London and New York: Routledge 1993.

New Casebooks: 'Antony and Cleopatra': William Shakespeare, ed. John Drakakis. Basingstoke: Macmillan, 1994.

Anne Barton: *Essays, Mainly Shakespearean*. Cambridge: Cambridge University Press, 1994.

Geoffrey Miles: *Shakespeare and the Constant Romans*. Oxford: Oxford University Press, 1996.

Shakespeare: The Roman Plays, ed. Graham Holderness, Bryan Loughrey and Andrew Murphy. Harlow: Longman, 1996.

Coppélia Kahn: *Roman Shakespeare: Warriors, Wounds and Women*. London: Routledge, 1997.

Kenneth Parker: *William Shakespeare: 'Antony and Cleopatra'*. Tavistock: Northcote House, 2000.

The Cambridge Companion to Shakespeare on Film, ed. Russell Jackson. Cambridge: Cambridge University Press, 2000.

John Sutherland and Cedric Watts: *Henry V, War Criminal? and Other Shakespeare Puzzles*. Oxford: Oxford University Press, 2000.

The Cambridge Companion to Shakespeare, ed. Margreta de Grazia and Stanley Wells. Cambridge: Cambridge University Press, 2001.

Shakespeare: An Oxford Guide, ed. Stanley Wells and Lena Cowen Orlin. Oxford: Oxford University Press, 2003.

NOTE ON SHAKESPEARE

William Shakespeare was the son of a glover at Stratford-upon-Avon, and tradition gives his date of birth as 23 April, 1564; certainly, three days later, he was christened at the parish church. It is likely that he attended the local Grammar School but had no university education. Of his early career there is no record, though John Aubrey reports a claim that he was a rural schoolmaster. In 1582 Shakespeare married Anne Hathaway, with whom he had two daughters, Susanna and Judith, and a son, Hamnet, who died in 1596. How he became involved with the stage in London is uncertain, but by 1592 he was sufficiently established as a playwright to be criticised in print as a challengingly versatile 'upstart Crow'. He was a leading member of the Lord Chamberlain's company, which became the King's Men on the accession of James I in 1603. The players performed at a wide variety of locations: in the public theatre, at the royal court, in noblemen's houses, at colleges, and probably in the yards of inns. Being not only a playwright and an actor but also a 'sharer' (one of the owners of the company, entitled to a share of the profits), Shakespeare prospered greatly, as is proven by the numerous records of his financial transactions. Meanwhile, his sonnets expressed the poet's love for a beautiful young man and a 'dark lady'. Towards the end of his life, Shakespeare loosened his ties with London and retired to New Place, the large house in Stratford-upon-Avon which he had bought in 1597. He died on 23 April, 1616, and is buried in the place of his baptism, Holy Trinity Church. The earliest collected edition of his plays, the First Folio, was published in 1623, and its prefatory verse-tributes include Ben Jonson's famous declaration, 'He was not of an age, but for all time'.

ACKNOWLEDGEMENTS AND TEXTUAL MATTERS

The present Wordsworth Classics' edition of *Antony and Cleopatra* provides a newly-edited text which takes the First Folio as its basis. It supersedes the previous Wordsworth Classics' *Antony and Cleopatra* (2000, revised in 2004), which by arrangement used Dover Wilson's Cambridge text. I have consulted – and am indebted to – numerous editions of *Antony and Cleopatra*, notably those by: John Dover Wilson (London: Cambridge University Press, 1950; rpt., 1964); Peter Alexander ('The Tudor Shakespeare': London and Glasgow: Collins, 1951; rpt., 1966); M. R. Ridley ('The Arden Shakespeare': London: Methuen, 1954; rpt., 1965); Barbara Everett ('The Signet Classic Shakespeare': New York: New American Library, 1964); G. Blakemore Evans *et al.* (*The Riverside Shakespeare*: Boston: Houghton Mifflin, 1974); Stanley Wells and Gary Taylor (*The Complete Works: Compact Edition*: Oxford: Oxford University Press, 1988); David Bevington ('The New Cambridge Shakespeare': Cambridge: Cambridge University Press, 1990; rpt., 1992); Marvin Spevack (*A New Variorum Edition*: New York: Modern Language Association of America, 1990; rpt, 1991); John F. Andrews (London: Dent Everyman, 1993); Michael Neill (Oxford: Oxford University Press, 1994); John Wilders ('The New Arden Shakespeare': London: Routledge, 1995); and Stephen Greenblatt *et al.* (*The Norton Shakespeare*: New York and London: Norton, 1997). My Glossary substantially revises Dover Wilson's.

Antony and Cleopatra was probably written in or around 1606–8. It was registered in May 1608. The earliest extant text appears in the First Folio (F1), the first collected edition of Shakespeare's plays, prepared by two leading members of his company, John

Heminge (or Heminges) and Henry Condell. This was published in 1623, seven years after the playwright's death. The present edition of *Antony and Cleopatra* offers a practical compromise between the F1 version, Shakespeare's intentions (insofar as they can be reasonably inferred) and modern requirements. As is customary, I have modernised various spellings, some of the punctuation and some stage-directions (while occasionally adding new stage-directions). F1 renders Antony's name usually as 'Anthony', sometimes as 'Anthonie' and occasionally as 'Antony': for various reasons, particularly consistency with the usage in my edition of *Julius Cæsar*, I have preferred 'Antony'. Many of F1's abundant colons and round brackets are retained here. I use a dash to indicate not only an interruption to a statement (or the start of a non-consecutive statement) but also a change of direction when a speaker turns from one addressee to another. An acute accent marks a syllable which, though not stressed in current usage, is stressed in the Shakespearian metrical line (as in 'There would he anchor his aspéct, and die'), while a grave accent marks a normally-unsounded syllable which needs to be sounded in order to preserve the metre (as in 'thronèd gods'). The glossary explains archaisms and unfamiliar terms, while the annotations offer clarification of obscurities.

No edition of the play can claim to be definitive; but this one, which aims to reconcile fidelity, clarity and concise practicality, promises to be very useful.

THE TRAGEDY OF
ANTONY AND CLEOPATRA

CHARACTERS

MARK ANTONY *(Marcus Antonius)*.

OCTAVIUS CÆSAR. ⎱ *Triumvirs.*

LEPIDUS. ⎰

CLEOPATRA, *Queen of Egypt.*

CHARMIAN *and* IRAS, *Cleopatra's attendants.*

OCTAVIA, *sister of Octavius.*

POMPEY *(Sextus Pompeius).*

PACORUS.

DOMITIUS ENOBARBUS, DEMETRIUS, PHILO,
    VENTIDIUS, EROS, SCARRUS, RANNIUS, LUCILLIUS,
    SILLIUS, CANIDIUS *and* DERCETUS: *followers of Antony.*

MÆCENAS, AGRIPPA, DOLABELLA, PROCULEIUS,
    THIDIAS, TAURUS *and* GALLUS: *followers of Octavius.*

ALEXAS, DIOMEDES, MARDIAN *(a eunuch) and*
    SELEUCUS *(the treasurer): followers of Cleopatra.*

MENAS, MENECRATES *and* VARRIUS: *followers of Pompey.*

A SOOTHSAYER *(Lamprius),* an EGYPTIAN, *a singing* BOY,
    an AMBASSADOR *and a* CLOWN.

CAPTAINS, SOLDIERS, GUARDS, ATTENDANTS,
    MESSENGERS, EUNUCHS, MUSICIANS, SERVANTS,
    a SENTRY *and* WATCHMEN.

*Locations: Alexandria and its environs; Rome; Sicily;
    Athens; near Actium; the Middle East.*

ANTONY AND CLEOPATRA[1]

ACT I, SCENE I.

Alexandria. Inside Cleopatra's palace.

Enter DEMETRIUS *and* PHILO.

PHILO   Nay, but this dotage of our General's
O'erflows the measure: those his goodly eyes,
That o'er the files and musters of the war
Have glowed like plated Mars, now bend, now turn
The office and devotion of their view
Upon a tawny front.[2] His captain's heart,
Which in the scuffles of great fights hath burst
The buckles on his breast, reneges all temper,
And is become the bellows and the fan
To cool a gypsy's lust.

Flourish. Enter ANTONY, CLEOPATRA *(fanned by* EUNUCHS*),*
and her RETINUE *(including* LADIES*).*

                Look where they come: 10
Take but good note, and you shall see in him
The triple pillar of the world[3] transformed
Into a strumpet's fool. Behold and see.

CLEOPATRA [*to Antony:*] If it be love indeed, tell me how much.
ANTONY   There's beggary in the love that can be reckoned.
CLEOPATRA I'll set a bourn how far to be beloved.
ANTONY   Then must thou needs find out new heaven, new earth.[4]

Enter a MESSENGER.

MESSEN.   News, my good lord, from Rome.
ANTONY   Grates me: the sum.
CLEOPATRA Nay, hear them, Antony.
Fulvia perchance is angry; or who knows   20
If the scarce-bearded Cæsar have not sent
His pow'rful mandate to you: 'Do this, or this,
Take in that kingdom, and enfranchise that;
Perform't, or else we damn thee.'

ANTONY   How, my love?

CLEOPATRA 'Perchance'? Nay, and most like:
　　　　　You must not stay here longer, your dismission
　　　　　Is come from Cæsar; therefore hear it, Antony.
　　　　　Where's Fulvia's process? Cæsar's, I would say? Both?
　　　　　Call in the messengers. As I am Egypt's Queen,
　　　　　Thou blushest, Antony, and that blood of thine　　　30
　　　　　Is Cæsar's homager: else so thy cheek pays shame
　　　　　When shrill-tongued Fulvia scolds.[5] The messengers!

ANTONY　Let Rome in Tiber melt, and the wide arch
　　　　　Of the ranged empire fall! Here is my space.
　　　　　Kingdoms are clay; our dungy earth alike
　　　　　Feeds beast as man; the nobleness of life
　　　　　Is to do thus, [*They embrace.*] when such a mutual pair
　　　　　And such a twain can do't; in which I bind,
　　　　　On pain of punishment, the world to weet
　　　　　We stand up peerless.[6]

CLEOPATRA　　　　　　　　　Excellent falsehood!　　　40
　　　　　– Why did he marry Fulvia, and not love her?
　　　　　I'll seem the fool I am not. Antony
　　　　　Will be himself.[7]

ANTONY　　　　　　　　But stirred by Cleopatra.
　　　　　Now, for the love of Love and her soft hours,
　　　　　Let's not confound the time with conference harsh:
　　　　　There's not a minute of our lives should stretch
　　　　　Without some pleasure new. What sport tonight?

CLEOPATRA Hear the ambassadors.

ANTONY　　　　　　　　　Fie, wrangling Queen!
　　　　　Whom every thing becomes, to chide, to laugh,
　　　　　To weep; whose every passion fully strives　　　50
　　　　　To make itself, in thee, fair and admired!
　　　　　No messenger but thine; and all alone,
　　　　　Tonight, we'll wander through the streets, and note
　　　　　The qualities of people. Come, my Queen;
　　　　　Last night you did desire it. [*To the messenger:*] Speak not
　　　　　　　　　　　　　　　　　　to us. [*Exit messenger.*
　　　　　　　[*Exeunt Antony and Cleopatra with the retinue.*

DEMETR.　Is Cæsar with Antonius prized so slight?

PHILO　　Sir, sometimes, when he is not Antony,
　　　　　He comes too short of that great property

Which still should go with Antony.

DEMETR.   I am full sorry
That he approves the common liar, who   60
Thus speaks of him at Rome; but I will hope
Of better deeds tomorrow. Rest you happy.   [*Exeunt.*

SCENE 2.

Alexandria. Inside Cleopatra's palace.

Enter ENOBARBUS, RANNIUS, LUCILLIUS, CHARMIAN,
ALEXAS, IRAS, *a* SOOTHSAYER (*Lamprius*) *and* MARDIAN (*a eunuch*).

CHARMIAN Lord Alexas, sweet Alexas, most any thing Alexas, al-
            most most absolute Alexas, where's the soothsayer that
            you praised so to th'Queen? O that I knew this husband,
            which, you say, must charge his horns with garlands![8]
ALEXAS   Soothsayer!
SOOTH.   Your will?
CHARMIAN Is this the man? — Is't you, sir, that know things?
SOOTH.   In Nature's infinite book of secrecy
            A little I can read.
ALEXAS   [*to Charmian:*]   Show him your hand.

                                    [*Charmian extends her hand.*
ENOBARB. [*calling:*] Bring in the banquet quickly: wine enough   10
            Cleopatra's health to drink!

Enter SERVANTS, *who place wine, fruit, etc., and exeunt.*

CHARMIAN [*to soothsayer:*] Good sir, give me good fortune.
SOOTH.   I make not, but foresee.
CHARMIAN Pray then, foresee me one.
SOOTH.   You shall be yet far fairer than you are.
CHARMIAN [*to Iras:*] He means in flesh.
IRAS   No, you shall paint when you are old.[9]
CHARMIAN Wrinkles forbid!
ALEXAS   Vex not his prescience; be attentive.
CHARMIAN Hush!   20
SOOTH.   You shall be more beloving than beloved.
CHARMIAN I had rather heat my liver with drinking.[10]
ALEXAS   Nay, hear him.

CHARMIAN Good now, some excellent fortune! Let me be married
to three kings in a forenoon, and widow them all; let
me have a child at fifty, to whom Herod of Jewry may
do homage.[11] Find me to marry me with Octavius
Cæsar, and companion me with my mistress.

SOOTH.   You shall outlive the lady whom you serve.

CHARMIAN O excellent! I love long life better than figs.

SOOTH.   You have seen and proved a fairer former fortune   30
Than that which is to approach.

CHARMIAN Then belike my children shall have no names. Prithee,
how many boys and wenches must I have?

SOOTH.   If every of your wishes had a womb,
And fertile every wish, a million.

CHARMIAN Out, fool! I forgive thee for a witch.[12]

ALEXAS   You think none but your sheets are privy to your wishes.

CHARMIAN [to soothsayer:] Nay, come, tell Iras hers.

ALEXAS   We'll know all our fortunes.

ENOBARB. Mine, and most of our fortunes tonight, shall be drunk   40
to bed.

IRAS   [extending her hand:] There's a palm presages chastity, if
nothing else.

CHARMIAN E'en as the o'erflowing Nilus presageth famine.[13]

IRAS   Go, you wild bedfellow, you cannot soothsay.

CHARMIAN Nay, if an oily palm be not a fruitful prognostication, I
cannot scratch mine ear. Prithee, tell her but a worky-
day fortune.

SOOTH.   Your fortunes are alike.

IRAS   But how, but how? Give me particulars.   50

SOOTH.   I have said.

IRAS   Am I not an inch of fortune better than she?

CHARMIAN Well, if you were but an inch of fortune better than I,
where would you choose it?

IRAS   Not in my husband's nose.

CHARMIAN Our worser thoughts heavens mend! – Alexas, come. –
His fortune, his fortune. – O let him marry a woman
that cannot go, sweet Isis, I beseech thee; and let her die
too, and give him a worse, and let worse follow worse,
till the worst of all follow him laughing to his grave,   60
fifty-fold a cuckold! Good Isis, hear me this prayer,

though thou deny me a matter of more weight; good
Isis, I beseech thee!

IRAS   Amen; dear goddess, hear that prayer of the people. For,
as it is a heart-breaking to see a handsome man loose-
wived, so it is a deadly sorrow to behold a foul knave
uncuckolded: therefore, dear Isis, keep decorum, and
fortune him accordingly!

CHARMIAN Amen.

ALEXAS   Lo now, if it lay in their hands to make me a cuckold, 70
they would make themselves whores but they'd do't.

Enter CLEOPATRA.

ENOBARB. Hush! Here comes Antony.[14]

CHARMIAN   Not he, the Queen.

CLEOPATRA Saw you my lord?

ENOBARB. No, lady.

CLEOPATRA Was he not here?

CHARMIAN No, madam.

CLEOPATRA He was disposed to mirth, but on the sudden
A Roman thought hath struck him. – Enobarbus!

ENOBARB. Madam?

CLEOPATRA Seek him, and bring him hither.   [*Exit Enobarbus.* 80
                                  Where's Alexas?

ALEXAS   Here at your service. My lord approaches.

Enter ANTONY *with a* MESSENGER.

CLEOPATRA We will not look upon him: go with us.   [*Exeunt.*

MESSEN. Fulvia thy wife first came into the field.

ANTONY   Against my brother Lucius?

MESSEN. Ay;
But soon that war had end, and the time's state
Made friends of them, jointing their force 'gainst Cæsar,
Whose better issue in the war from Italy
Upon the first encounter drave them.

ANTONY   Well, what worst?

MESSEN. The nature of bad news infects the teller.   90

ANTONY   When it concerns the fool or coward. On.
Things that are past are done, with me. 'Tis thus:
Who tells me true, though in his tale lie death,
I hear him as he flattered.

MESSEN.   Labienus
          (This is stiff news) hath with his Parthian force
          Extended Asia: from Eúphratés
          His conquering banner shook, from Syria
          To Lydia and to Ionia,[15]
          Whilst —
ANTONY   'Antony', thou wouldst say —
MESSEN.   O my lord.
ANTONY   Speak to me home, mince not the general tongue,   100
          Name Cleopatra as she is called in Rome;
          Rail thou in Fulvia's phrase, and taunt my faults
          With such full licence as both truth and malice
          Have power to utter. O then we bring forth weeds
          When our quick minds lie still, and our ills told us
          Is as our earing. Fare thee well awhile.
MESSEN.   At your noble pleasure.   [Exit messenger.

                    Enter MESSENGERS 2 and 3.

ANTONY   From Sicyon, how the news? Speak there.
MESSEN. 2 The man from Sicyon, is there such an one?
MESSEN. 3 He stays upon your will.   110
ANTONY   Let him appear.
                              [Exeunt messengers.

          These strong Egyptian fetters I must break,
          Or lose myself in dotage.

               Enter MESSENGER 4, holding a letter.

                              — What are you?

MESSEN. 4 Fulvia thy wife is dead.
ANTONY   Where died she?
MESSEN. 4 In Sicyon.[16]
          Her length of sickness, with what else more serious
          Importeth thee to know, this bears. [He gives him a letter.
ANTONY   Forbear me.
                              [Exit messenger.

          There's a great spirit gone! Thus did I desire it.
          What our contempts doth often hurl from us,
          We wish it ours again. The present pleasure,
          By revolution lowering, does become   120
          The opposite of itself:[17] she's good, being gone;

The hand could pluck her back that shoved her on.
I must from this enchanting queen break off:
Ten thousand harms, more than the ills I know,
My idleness doth hatch. – How now, Enobarbus!

Enter ENOBARBUS.

ENOBARB. What's your pleasure, sir?

ANTONY   I must with haste from hence.

ENOBARB. Why then we kill all our women. We see how mortal
an unkindness is to them: if they suffer our departure,
death's the word.   130

ANTONY   I must be gone.

ENOBARB. Under a compelling occasion, let women die. It were
pity to cast them away for nothing; though, between
them and a great cause, they should be esteemed nothing. Cleopatra, catching but the least noise of this, dies
instantly: I have seen her die twenty times upon far
poorer moment: I do think there is mettle in death,
which commits some loving act upon her, she hath such
a celerity in dying.

ANTONY   She is cunning past man's thought.   140

ENOBARB. Alack sir, no; her passions are made of nothing but the
finest part of pure love. We cannot call her winds and
waters 'sighs and tears'; they are greater storms and
tempests than almanacs can report. This cannot be
cunning in her; if it be, she makes a shower of rain as
well as Jove.[18]

ANTONY   Would I had never seen her!

ENOBARB. O sir, you had then left unseen a wonderful piece of
work, which not to have been blest withal would have
discredited your travel.   150

ANTONY   Fulvia is dead.

ENOBARB. Sir?

ANTONY   Fulvia is dead.

ENOBARB. Fulvia?

ANTONY   Dead.

ENOBARB. Why sir, give the gods a thankful sacrifice. When it
pleaseth their deities to take the wife of a man from him,
it shows to man the tailors of the earth;[19] comforting
therein, that when old robes are worn out, there are

members to make new. If there were no more women 160
but Fulvia, then had you indeed a cut, and the case to be
lamented.[20] This grief is crowned with consolation:
your old smock brings forth a new petticoat, and indeed
the tears live in an onion that should water this sorrow.

ANTONY   The business she hath broachèd in the state
Cannot endure my absence.

ENOBARB.   And the business you have broached here cannot be
without you; especially that of Cleopatra's, which wholly
depends on your abode.[21]

ANTONY   No more light answers. Let our officers 170
Have notice what we purpose. I shall break
The cause of our expedience to the Queen,
And get her leave to part. For not alone
The death of Fulvia, with more urgent touches,
Do strongly speak to us, but the letters too
Of many our contriving friends in Rome
Petition us at home. Sextus Pompeius
Hath given the dare to Cæsar, and commands
The empire of the sea. Our slippery people,
Whose love is never linked to the deserver 180
Till his deserts are past, begin to throw
Pompey the Great and all his dignities
Upon his son,[22] who, high in name and power,
Higher than both in blood and life, stands up
For the main soldier; whose quality, going on,
The sides o'th'world may danger.[23] Much is breeding,
Which, like the courser's hair, hath yet but life
And not a serpent's poison.[24] Say our pleasure,
To such whose place is under us, requires
Our quick remove from hence. 190

ENOBARB.   I shall do't.   [*Exeunt separately.*

SCENE 3.

Alexandria. Inside Cleopatra's palace.

Enter CLEOPATRA, CHARMIAN, ALEXAS *and* IRAS.

CLEOPATRA Where is he?

CHARMIAN   I did not see him since.

CLEOPATRA [*to Alexas:*] See where he is, who's with him, what he does.
I did not send you. If you find him sad,
Say I am dancing; if in mirth, report
That I am sudden sick. Quick, and return. [*Exit Alexas.*

CHARMIAN Madam, methinks, if you did love him dearly,
You do not hold the method to enforce
The like from him.

CLEOPATRA   What should I do, I do not?

CHARMIAN In each thing give him way, cross him in nothing.

CLEOPATRA Thou teachest, like a fool, the way to lose him.   10

CHARMIAN Tempt him not so too far. I wish, forbear;
In time we hate that which we often fear.

Enter ANTONY.

But here comes Antony.

CLEOPATRA   I am sick and sullen.

ANTONY I am sorry to give breathing to my purpose —

CLEOPATRA Help me away, dear Charmian; I shall fall.
It cannot be thus long; the sides of nature
Will not sustain it.

ANTONY   Now, my dearest Queen —

CLEOPATRA Pray you, stand farther from me.

ANTONY   What's the matter?

CLEOPATRA I know, by that same eye, there's some good news.
What, says the married woman you may go?   20
Would she had never given you leave to come!
Let her not say 'tis I that keep you here.
I have no power upon you: hers you are.

ANTONY The gods best know —

CLEOPATRA   O never was there queen
So mightily betrayed! Yet at the first
I saw the treasons planted.

ANTONY   Cleopatra —

CLEOPATRA Why should I think you can be mine and true
          (Though you in swearing shake the thronèd gods),
          Who have been false to Fulvia? Riotous madness,
          To be entangled with those mouth-made vows,   30
          Which break themselves in swearing!

ANTONY   Most sweet Queen —

CLEOPATRA Nay, pray you, seek no colour for your going,
          But bid farewell, and go: when you sued staying,
          Then was the time for words. No going then;
          Eternity was in our lips and eyes,
          Bliss in our brows' bent; none our parts so poor
          But was a race of heaven. They are so still,
          Or thou, the greatest soldier of the world,
          Art turned the greatest liar.

ANTONY   How now, lady?

CLEOPATRA I would I had thy inches; thou shouldst know   40
          There were a heart in Egypt.[25]

ANTONY   Hear me, Queen:
          The strong necessity of time commands
          Our services a while; but my full heart
          Remains in use with you. Our Italy
          Shines o'er with civil swords: Sextus Pompeius
          Makes his approaches to the port of Rome:
          Equality of two domestic powers
          Breed scrupulous faction. The hated, grown to strength,
          Are newly grown to love. The condemned Pompey,
          Rich in his father's honour, creeps apace   50
          Into the hearts of such as have not thrived
          Upon the present state, whose numbers threaten;
          And quietness, grown sick of rest, would purge
          By any desperate change. My more particular,
          And that which most with you should safe my going,
          Is Fulvia's death.

CLEOPATRA Though age from folly could not give me freedom,
          It does from childishness. Can Fulvia die?

ANTONY   She's dead, my Queen.   [*He offers letters to her.*
          Look here, and at thy sovereign leisure read   60
          The garboils she awaked: at the last, best;

    See when and where she died.

CLEOPATRA   O most false love!
Where be the sacred vials thou shouldst fill
With sorrowful water? Now I see, I see,
In Fulvia's death, how mine received shall be.

ANTONY   Quarrel no more, but be prepared to know
The purposes I bear; which are, or cease,
As you shall give th'advice. By the fire
That quickens Nilus' slime, I go from hence
Thy soldier, servant, making peace or war   70
As thou affects.

CLEOPATRA   Cut my lace, Charmian, come.
But let it be: I am quickly ill, and well,
So Antony loves.

ANTONY   My precious Queen, forbear;
And give true evidence to his love, which stands
An honourable trial.

CLEOPATRA   So Fulvia told me.
I prithee, turn aside and weep for her,
Then bid adieu to me, and say the tears
Belong to Egypt. Good now, play one scene
Of excellent dissembling, and let it look
Like perfect honour.

ANTONY   You'll heat my blood no more!   80

CLEOPATRA You can do better yet; but this is meetly.

ANTONY   Now, by my sword –

CLEOPATRA   And target. Still he mends.
But this is not the best. Look, prithee, Charmian,
How this Hercúlean Roman does become
The carriage of his chafe.[26]

ANTONY   I'll leave you, lady.

CLEOPATRA   Courteous lord, one word.
Sir, you and I must part – but that's not it.
Sir, you and I have loved – but there's not it;
That you know well. Something it is I would . . .
O, my oblivion is a very Antony,   90
And I am all forgotten.[27]

ANTONY   But that your royalty
Holds idleness your subject, I should take you

For idleness itself.

CLEOPATRA 'Tis sweating labour,
To bear such idleness so near the heart
As Cleopatra this.[28] But, sir, forgive me,
Since my becomings kill me when they do not
Eye well to you. Your honour calls you hence;
Therefore be deaf to my unpitied folly,
And all the gods go with you! Upon your sword
Sit laurel victory, and smooth success   100
Be strewed before your feet!

ANTONY Let us go. Come;
Our separation so abides and flies,
That thou, residing here, goes yet with me,
And I, hence fleeting, here remain with thee.
Away!   [*Exeunt.*

SCENE 4.

Rome. Inside Cæsar's house.

Enter OCTAVIUS CÆSAR *(reading a letter),* LEPIDUS, *and their* RETINUE.

CÆSAR You may see, Lepidus, and henceforth know,
It is not Cæsar's natural vice to hate
Our great competitor. From Alexandria
This is the news: he fishes, drinks, and wastes
The lamps of night in revel: is not more manlike
Than Cleopatra, nor the Queen of Ptolemy[29]
More womanly than he: hardly gave audience, or
Vouchsafed to think he had partners. You shall
find there
A man who is the abstract of all faults
That all men follow.

LEPIDUS I must not think there are   10
Evils enow to darken all his goodness:
His faults, in him, seem as the spots of heaven,
More fiery by night's blackness; hereditary,
Rather than purchased; what he cannot change,
Than what he chooses.

CÆSAR You are too indulgent. Let's grant it is not

Amiss to tumble on the bed of Ptolemy,
To give a kingdom for a mirth, to sit
And keep the turn of tippling with a slave,
To reel the streets at noon, and stand the buffet   20
With knaves that smell of sweat. Say this becomes him
(As his composure must be rare indeed,
Whom these things cannot blemish), yet must Antony
No way excuse his foils, when we do bear
So great weight in his lightness.[30] If he filled
His vacancy with his voluptuousness,
Full surfeits and the dryness of his bones
Call on him for't; but to confound such time
That drums him from his sport and speaks as loud
As his own state and ours, 'tis to be chid [31]   30
As we rate boys who, being mature in knowledge,
Pawn their experience to their present pleasure,
And so rebel to judgement.

Enter a MESSENGER.

LEPIDUS   Here's more news.
MESSEN.   Thy biddings have been done, and every hour,
Most noble Cæsar, shalt thou have report
How 'tis abroad. Pompey is strong at sea,
And, it appears, he is belov'd of those
That only have feared Cæsar: to the ports
The discontents repair, and men's reports
Give him much wronged.

CÆSAR   I should have known no less: 40
It hath been taught us from the primal state
That he which is was wished until he were;
And the ebbed man, ne'er loved till ne'er worth love,
Comes deared by being lacked.[32] This common body,
Like to a vagabond flag upon the stream,
Goes to and back, lackeying the varying tide,
To rot itself with motion.

MESSEN.   Cæsar, I bring thee word
Menecrates and Menas, famous pirates,
Make the sea serve them, which they ear and wound
With keels of every kind. Many hot inroads   50
They make in Italy; the borders maritime

	Lack blood to think on't, and flush youth revolt;	
	No vessel can peep forth, but 'tis as soon	
	Taken as seen: for Pompey's name strikes more	
	Than could his war resisted.[33]	
CÆSAR	Antony,	
	Leave thy lascivious wassails. When thou once	
	Was beaten from Modena, where thou slew'st	
	Hirtius and Pansa, consuls, at thy heel	
	Did famine follow, whom thou fought'st against	
	(Though daintily brought up) with patience more	60
	Than savages could suffer. Thou didst drink	
	The stale of horses and the gilded puddle	
	Which beasts would cough at. Thy palate then did deign	
	The roughest berry on the rudest hedge;	
	Yea, like the stag when snow the pasture sheets,	
	The barks of trees thou browsèd. On the Alps,	
	It is reported, thou didst eat strange flesh,	
	Which some did die to look on. And all this	
	(It wounds thine honour that I speak it now)	
	Was borne so like a soldier that thy cheek	70
	So much as lanked not.	
LEPIDUS	'Tis pity of him.	
CÆSAR	Let his shames quickly	
	Drive him to Rome. 'Tis time we twain	
	Did show ourselves i'th'field, and to that end	
	Assemble we immediate council. Pompey	
	Thrives in our idleness.	
LEPIDUS	Tomorrow, Cæsar,	
	I shall be furnished to inform you rightly	
	Both what by sea and land I can be able	
	To front this present time.	
CÆSAR	Till which encounter,	
	It is my business too. Farewell.	80
LEPIDUS	Farewell, my lord. What you shall know meantime	
	Of stirs abroad, I shall beseech you, sir,	
	To let me be partaker.	
CÆSAR	Doubt not, sir;	
	I knew it for my bond. [Exeunt.	

SCENE 5.

Alexandria. Inside Cleopatra's palace.

Enter CLEOPATRA, CHARMIAN, IRAS *and* MARDIAN.

CLEOPATRA Charmian.

CHARMIAN Madam?

CLEOPATRA [*yawning:*] Ha . . . ha. Give me to drink mandragora.

CHARMIAN Why, madam?

CLEOPATRA That I might sleep out this great gap of time:
    My Antony is away.

CHARMIAN You think of him too much.

CLEOPATRA O 'tis treason!

CHARMIAN   Madam, I trust not so.

CLEOPATRA Thou, eunuch Mardian!

MARDIAN   What's your Highness' pleasure?

CLEOPATRA Not now to hear thee sing. I take no pleasure   10
    In aught an eunuch has. 'Tis well for thee
    That, being unseminared, thy freer thoughts
    May not fly forth of Egypt. Hast thou affections?

MARDIAN Yes, gracious madam.

CLEOPATRA Indeed?

MARDIAN Not in deed, madam, for I can do nothing
    But what indeed is honest to be done;
    Yet have I fierce affections, and think
    What Venus did with Mars.[34]

CLEOPATRA   O Charmian,
    Where think'st thou he is now? Stands he, or sits he?   20
    Or does he walk? Or is he on his horse?
    O happy horse, to bear the weight of Antony!
    Do bravely, horse; for wot'st thou whom thou mov'st?
    The demi-Atlas of this earth, the arm
    And burgonet of men.[35] He's speaking now,
    Or murmuring 'Where's my serpent of old Nile?'
    (For so he calls me): now I feed myself
    With most delicious poison. Think on me,
    That am with Phœbus' amorous pinches black,[36]

And wrinkled deep in time. Broad-fronted Cæsar,   30
When thou wast here above the ground, I was
A morsel for a monarch; and great Pompey
Would stand and make his eyes grow in my brow:
There would he anchor his aspéct, and die
With looking on his life.[37]

Enter ALEXAS.

ALEXAS   Sovereign of Egypt, hail!
CLEOPATRA How much unlike art thou Mark Antony!
          Yet, coming from him, that great med'cine hath
          With his tinct gilded thee.
          How goes it with my brave Mark Antony?
ALEXAS   Last thing he did (dear Queen),   40
          He kissed – the last of many doubled kisses –
          This orient pearl. His speech sticks in my heart.
CLEOPATRA Mine ear must pluck it thence.
ALEXAS   'Good friend,' quoth he,
          'Say, the firm Roman to great Egypt sends
          This treasure of an oyster; at whose foot,
          To mend the petty present, I will piece
          Her opulent throne with kingdoms. All the East,
          (Say thou) shall call her mistress.' So he nodded,
          And soberly did mount an arm-gaunt steed,
          Who neighed so high that what I would have spoke   50
          Was beastly dumbed by him.
CLEOPATRA What was he, sad or merry?
ALEXAS   Like to the time o'th'year between the extremes
          Of hot and cold, he was nor sad nor merry.
CLEOPATRA O well-divided disposition! Note him,
          Note him, good Charmian, 'tis the man; but note him:
          He was not sad, for he would shine on those
          That make their looks by his; he was not merry,
          Which seemed to tell them his remembrance lay
          In Egypt with his joy; but between both.   60
          O heavenly mingle! Be'st thou sad or merry,
          The violence of either thee becomes,
          So does it no man else. Met'st thou my posts?
ALEXAS   Ay, madam, twenty several messengers:

      Why do you send so thick?

CLEOPATRA   Who's born that day
When I forget to send to Antony,
Shall die a beggar. – Ink and paper, Charmian. –
Welcome, my good Alexas. – Did I, Charmian,
Ever love Cæsar so?

CHARMIAN   O that brave Cæsar!

CLEOPATRA Be choked with such another emphasis!   70
Say, 'The brave Antony'.

CHARMIAN   The valiant Cæsar.

CLEOPATRA By Isis, I will give thee bloody teeth,
If thou with Cæsar paragon again
My man of men.

CHARMIAN   By your most gracious pardon,
I sing but after you.

CLEOPATRA   My salad days,
When I was green in judgement, cold in blood,
To say as I said then. But come, away;
Get me ink and paper.
He shall have every day a several greeting,
Or I'll unpeople Egypt.   [*Exeunt.* 80

ACT 2, SCENE 1.

Sicily. Inside Pompey's house.

Enter POMPEY, MENECRATES *and* MENAS *'in warlike manner'.*[38]

POMPEY   If the great gods be just, they shall assist
The deeds of justest men.

MENEC.   Know, worthy Pompey,
That what they do delay, they not deny.

POMPEY   Whiles we are suitors to their throne, decays
The thing we sue for.

MENEC.   We, ignorant of ourselves,
Beg often our own harms, which the wise pow'rs
Deny us for our good; so find we profit
By losing of our prayers.

POMPEY   I shall do well:
The people love me, and the sea is mine;
My powers are crescent, and my auguring hope   10
Says it will come to th'full. Mark Antony
In Egypt sits at dinner, and will make
No wars without doors. Cæsar gets money where
He loses hearts. Lepidus flatters both,
Of both is flattered; but he neither loves,
Nor either cares for him.

MENAS   Cæsar and Lepidus
Are in the field: a mighty strength they carry.

POMPEY   Where have you this? 'Tis false.

MENAS   From Silvius, sir.

POMPEY   He dreams: I know they are in Rome together,
Looking for Antony. But all the charms of love,   20
Salt Cleopatra, soften thy waned lip;
Let witchcraft join with beauty, lust with both;
Tie up the libertine in a field of feasts;
Keep his brain fuming. Epicurean cooks,
Sharpen with cloyless sauce his appetite,
That sleep and feeding may prorogue his honour,
Even till a Letheed dulness —

Enter VARRIUS.

                  How now, Varrius?

VARRIUS   This is most certain that I shall deliver:
Mark Antony is every hour in Rome
Expected: since he went from Egypt 'tis   30
A space for farther travel.

POMPEY   I could have given less matter
A better ear. Menas, I did not think
This amorous surfeiter would have donned his helm
For such a petty war. His soldiership
Is twice the other twain. But let us rear
The higher our opinion, that our stirring
Can from the lap of Egypt's widow pluck
The ne'er-lust-wearied Antony.

MENAS   I cannot hope
Cæsar and Antony shall well greet together.   40
His wife that's dead did trespasses to Cæsar;
His brother warred upon him; although, I think,
Not moved by Antony.

POMPEY   I know not, Menas,
How lesser enmities may give way to greater.
Were't not that we stand up against them all,
'Twere pregnant they should square between
                      themselves,
For they have entertainèd cause enough
To draw their swords; but how the fear of us
May cément their divisions, and bind up
The petty difference, we yet not know.   50
Be't as our gods will have't; it only stands
Our lives upon, to use our strongest hands.[39]
Come, Menas.   [*Exeunt.*

SCENE 2.

Rome. Inside the house of Lepidus.

Enter ENOBARBUS *and* LEPIDUS.

LEPIDUS   Good Enobarbus, 'tis a worthy deed,
           And shall become you well, to entreat your captain
           To soft and gentle speech.

ENOBARB.   I shall entreat him
           To answer like himself: if Cæsar move him,
           Let Antony look over Cæsar's head,
           And speak as loud as Mars. By Jupiter,
           Were I the wearer of Antonio's beard,
           I would not shave't today.⁴⁰

LEPIDUS   'Tis not a time
           For private stomaching.

ENOBARB.   Every time
           Serves for the matter that is then born in't.   10

LEPIDUS   But small to greater matters must give way.

ENOBARB.   Not if the small come first.

LEPIDUS   Your speech is passion:
           But, pray you, stir no embers up. Here comes
           The noble Antony.

           Enter, conversing, ANTONY *and* VENTIDIUS.

ENOBARB.   And yonder, Cæsar.

           Enter, conversing, CÆSAR, MÆCENAS *and* AGRIPPA.

ANTONY   If we compose well here, to Parthia:
           Hark, Ventidius.

CÆSAR   I do not know, Mæcenas; ask Agrippa.

LEPIDUS   [*to Cæsar and Antony:*] Noble friends:
           That which combined us was most great, and let not
           A leaner action rend us. What's amiss,   20
           May it be gently heard. When we debate
           Our trivial difference loud, we do commit
           Murder in healing wounds. Then, noble partners,
           The rather for I earnestly beseech,
           Touch you the sourest points with sweetest terms,

Nor curstness grow to th'matter.

ANTONY   'Tis spoken well.
Were we before our armies and to fight,
I should do thus.41   [Flourish.

CÆSAR   Welcome to Rome.

ANTONY   Thank you.   30

CÆSAR   Sit.

ANTONY   Sit, sir.

CÆSAR   Nay, then.   [They sit.

ANTONY   I learn, you take things ill which are not so;
Or being, concern you not.

CÆSAR   I must be laughed at,
If, or for nothing or a little, I
Should say myself offended, and with you
Chiefly i'th'world; more laughed at, that I should
Once name you derogately, when to sound your name
It not concerned me.   40

ANTONY   My being in Egypt, Cæsar, what was't to you?

CÆSAR   No more than my residing here at Rome
Might be to you in Egypt; yet, if you there
Did practise on my state, your being in Egypt
Might be my question.

ANTONY   How intend you, 'practised'?

CÆSAR   You may be pleased to catch at mine intent
By what did here befall me. Your wife and brother
Made wars upon me, and their contestation
Was then for you: you were the word of war.

ANTONY   You do mistake your business. My brother never   50
Did urge me in his act: I did inquire it,
And have my learning from some true reports
That drew their swords with you. Did he not rather
Discredit my authority with yours,
And make the wars alike against my stomach,
Having alike your cause? Of this my letters
Before did satisfy you. If you'll patch a quarrel,
As matter whole you have to make it with,
It must not be with this.42

CÆSAR   You praise yourself
By laying defects of judgement to me, but   60

You patched up your excuses.

ANTONY   Not so, not so.
I know you could not lack, I am certain on't,
Very necessity of this thought,[43] that I,
Your partner in the cause 'gainst which he fought,
Could not with graceful eyes attend those wars
Which fronted mine own peace. As for my wife,
I would you had her spirit in such another:
The third o'th'world is yours, which with a snaffle
You may pace easy, but not such a wife –

ENOBARB. Would we had all such wives, that the men might go   70
to wars with the women –

ANTONY So much uncurbable; her garboils, Cæsar,
Made out of her impatience (which not wanted
Shrewdness of policy too), I grieving grant
Did you too much disquiet: for that you must
But say, I could not help it.

CÆSAR   I wrote to you:
When rioting in Alexandria, you
Did pocket up my letters, and with taunts
Did gibe my missive out of audience.

ANTONY   Sir,
He fell upon me, ere admitted, then;   80
Three kings I had newly feasted, and did want
Of what I was i'th'morning: but next day
I told him of myself, which was as much
As to have asked him pardon. Let this fellow
Be nothing of our strife: if we contend,
Out of our question wipe him.

CÆSAR   You have broken
The article of your oath, which you shall never
Have tongue to charge me with.

LEPIDUS   Soft, Cæsar!

ANTONY No, Lepidus, let him speak:
The honour is sacred which he talks on now,   90
Supposing that I lacked it. But on, Cæsar:
The article of my oath –

CÆSAR To lend me arms and aid when I required them,
The which you both denied.

ANTONY   Neglected, rather;
And then when poisoned hours had bound me up
From mine own knowledge. As nearly as I may,
I'll play the penitent to you; but mine honesty
Shall not make poor my greatness, nor my power
Work without it. Truth is, that Fulvia,
To have me out of Egypt, made wars here;   100
For which myself, the ignorant motive, do
So far ask pardon as befits mine honour
To stoop in such a case.

LEPIDUS   'Tis noble spoken.

MÆCENAS   If it might please you to enforce no further
The griefs between ye, to forget them quite
Were to remember that the present need
Speaks to atone you.

LEPIDUS   Worthily spoken, Mæcenas.

ENOBARB.   Or, if you borrow one another's love for the instant,
you may, when you hear no more words of Pompey,
return it again: you shall have time to wrangle in, when   110
you have nothing else to do.

ANTONY   Thou art a soldier only: speak no more.

ENOBARB.   That truth should be silent, I had almost forgot.

ANTONY   You wrong this presence; therefore speak no more.

ENOBARB.   Go to then: your considerate stone.

CÆSAR   I do not much dislike the matter, but
The manner of his speech; for't cannot be
We shall remain in friendship, our conditions
So differing in their acts.[44] Yet, if I knew
What hoop should hold us staunch from edge to edge   120
O'th'world, I would pursue it.

AGRIPPA   Give me leave, Cæsar.

CÆSAR   Speak, Agrippa.

AGRIPPA   Thou hast a sister by the mother's side,
Admired Octavia.[45] Great Mark Antony
Is now a widower.

CÆSAR   Say not so, Agrippa:
If Cleopatra heard you, your reproof
Were well deserved of rashness.

ANTONY   I am not married, Cæsar: let me hear

Agrippa further speak.

AGRIPPA To hold you in perpetual amity,   130
To make you brothers, and to knit your hearts
With an unslipping knot, take Antony
Octavia to his wife: whose beauty claims
No worse a husband than the best of men;
Whose virtue and whose general graces speak
That which none else can utter. By this marriage,
All little jealousies which now seem great,
And all great fears which now import their dangers,
Would then be nothing. Truths would be tales,
Where now half tales be truths; her love to both   140
Would each to other, and all loves to both,
Draw after her. Pardon what I have spoke,
For 'tis a studied, not a present thought,
By duty ruminated.

ANTONY   Will Cæsar speak?

CÆSAR Not till he hears how Antony is touched
With what is spoke already.

ANTONY What power is in Agrippa,
If I would say, 'Agrippa, be it so',
To make this good?

CÆSAR   The power of Cæsar, and
His power unto Octavia.

ANTONY   May I never   150
To this good purpose, that so fairly shows,
Dream of impediment! Let me have thy hand:
Further this act of grace; and, from this hour,
The heart of brothers govern in our loves
And sway our great designs!

CÆSAR [clasping Antony's hand:]   There's my hand.
A sister I bequeath you, whom no brother
Did ever love so dearly. Let her live
To join our kingdoms and our hearts; and never
Fly off our loves again!

LEPIDUS   Happily, amen!

ANTONY I did not think to draw my sword 'gainst Pompey,   160
For he hath laid strange courtesies and great
Of late upon me. I must thank him only,

Lest my remembrance suffer ill report;
At heel of that, defy him.

LEPIDUS   Time calls upon's:
Of us must Pompey presently be sought,
Or else he seeks out us.

ANTONY   Where lies he?

CÆSAR   About the Mount Misena.

ANTONY   What is his strength
By land?

CÆSAR   Great and increasing: but by sea
He is an absolute master.

ANTONY   So is the fame.
Would we had spoke together! Haste we for it.   170
Yet, ere we put ourselves in arms, dispatch we
The business we have talked of.

CÆSAR   With most gladness;
And do invite you to my sister's view,
Whither straight I'll lead you.

ANTONY   Let us, Lepidus,
Not lack your company.

LEPIDUS   Noble Antony,
Not sickness should detain me.

     [*Flourish. Exeunt Cæsar, Antony, Lepidus and Ventidius.*

MÆCENAS   [*to Enobarbus:*] Welcome from Egypt, sir.

ENOBARB.   Half the heart of Cæsar, worthy Mæcenas! My honourable friend, Agrippa!

AGRIPPA   Good Enobarbus!   180

MÆCENAS   We have cause to be glad that matters are so well digested.
You stayed well by't in Egypt.

ENOBARB.   Ay, sir; we did sleep day out of countenance, and made
the night light with drinking.

MÆCENAS   Eight wild boars roasted whole at a breakfast, and but
twelve persons there: is this true?

ENOBARB.   This was but as a fly by an eagle: we had much more
monstrous matter of feast, which worthily deserved
noting.

MÆCENAS   She's a most triumphant lady, if report be square to her.   190

ENOBARB.   When she first met Mark Antony, she pursed up his heart
upon the river of Cydnus.

AGRIPPA   There she appeared indeed; or my reporter devised well
         for her.

ENOBARB.   I will tell you.
       The barge she sat in, like a burnished throne,
       Burnt on the water: the poop was beaten gold;
       Purple the sails, and so perfumèd that
       The winds were love-sick with them; the oars
                                         were silver,
       Which to the tune of flutes kept stroke, and made   200
       The water which they beat to follow faster,
       As amorous of their strokes. For her own person,
       It beggared all description. She did lie
       In her pavilion, cloth-of-gold, of tissue,
       O'er-picturing that Venus where we see
       The fancy out-work nature. On each side her
       Stood pretty dimpled boys, like smiling Cupids,
       With divers-coloured fans, whose wind did seem
       To glow the delicate cheeks which they did cool,
       And what they undid did.

AGRIPPA   O rare for Antony!   210

ENOBARB.   Her gentlewomen, like the Nereides,
       So many mermaids, tended her i'th'eyes,
       And made their bends adornings.[46] At the helm,
       A seeming mermaid steers: the silken tackle
       Swell with the touches of those flower-soft hands,
       That yarely frame the office. From the barge
       A strange invisible perfume hits the sense
       Of the adjacent wharfs. The city cast
       Her people out upon her; and Antony,
       Enthroned i'th'market-place, did sit alone,   220
       Whistling to th'air; which, but for vacancy,
       Had gone to gaze on Cleopatra too,
       And made a gap in nature.[47]

AGRIPPA   Rare Egyptian!

ENOBARB.   Upon her landing, Antony sent to her,
       Invited her to supper: she replied,
       It should be better he became her guest;
       Which she entreated. Our courteous Antony,
       Whom ne'er the word of 'No' woman heard speak,

       Being barbered ten times o'er, goes to the feast,
       And, for his ordinary, pays his heart   230
       For what his eyes eat only.[48]

AGRIPPA   Royal wench!
       She made great Cæsar lay his sword to bed:
       He ploughed her, and she cropped.[49]

ENOBARB.   I saw her once
       Hop forty paces through the public street;
       And having lost her breath, she spoke, and panted,
       That she did make defect perfection,
       And, breathless, pow'r breathe forth.

MÆCENAS Now Antony must leave her utterly.

ENOBARB. Never; he will not.
       Age cannot wither her, nor custom stale   240
       Her infinite variety: other women cloy
       The appetites they feed, but she makes hungry
       Where most she satisfies; for vilest things
       Become themselves in her, that the holy priests
       Bless her when she is riggish.

MÆCENAS If beauty, wisdom, modesty, can settle
       The heart of Antony, Octavia is
       A blessèd lottery to him.

AGRIPPA   Let us go.
       Good Enobarbus, make yourself my guest
       Whilst you abide here.

ENOBARB.   Humbly, sir, I thank you.   250
                                   [*Exeunt.*

SCENE 3.

Rome. Inside Cæsar's house.

Enter ANTONY *and* CÆSAR, *with* OCTAVIA *between them.*

ANTONY   The world, and my great office, will sometimes
            Divide me from your bosom.

OCTAVIA   All which time
            Before the gods my knee shall bow in prayers
            To them for you.

ANTONY   – Good night, sir. – My Octavia,
            Read not my blemishes in the world's report:
            I have not kept my square, but that to come
            Shall all be done by th'rule. Good night, dear lady.

OCTAVIA   Good night, sir.

CÆSAR   Good night.   [*Exeunt Cæsar with Octavia.*

Enter the SOOTHSAYER.

ANTONY   Now, sirrah: you do wish yourself in Egypt?   10

SOOTH.   Would I had never come from thence, nor you thither.

ANTONY   If you can, your reason?

SOOTH.   I see it in my motion, have it not in my tongue; but yet
            hie you to Egypt again.

ANTONY   Say to me, whose fortunes shall rise higher, Cæsar's or
            mine?

SOOTH.   Cæsar's.
            Therefore, O Antony, stay not by his side.
            Thy dæmon, that thy spirit which keeps thee, is
            Noble, courageous, high, unmatchable,   20
            Where Cæsar's is not. But near him, thy angel
            Becomes afeard, as being o'erpow'red; therefore
            Make space enough between you.

ANTONY   Speak this no more.

SOOTH.   To none but thee; no more but when to thee.
            If thou dost play with him at any game,
            Thou art sure to lose; and, of that natural luck,
            He beats thee 'gainst the odds. Thy lustre thickens,
            When he shines by. I say again, thy spirit

Is all afraid to govern thee near him;
But he away, 'tis noble.

ANTONY   Get thee gone: 30
Say to Ventidius I would speak with him. [*Exit soothsayer.*
– He shall to Parthia. – Be it art or hap,
He hath spoken true. The very dice obey him,
And in our sports my better cunning faints
Under his chance; if we draw lots, he speeds;
His cocks do win the battle still of mine
When it is all to nought, and his quails ever
Beat mine, inhooped, at odds.⁵⁰ I will to Egypt;
And though I make this marriage for my peace,
I'th'East my pleasure lies.

                    Enter VENTIDIUS.

                              O come, Ventidius: 40
You must to Parthia: your commission's ready;
Follow me, and receive't.   [*Exeunt.*

SCENE 4.

Rome. A street.

Enter LEPIDUS, MÆCENAS, *and* AGRIPPA.

LEPIDUS   Trouble yourselves no further: pray you, hasten
             Your generals after.
AGRIPPA   Sir, Mark Antony
             Will e'en but kiss Octavia, and we'll follow.
LEPIDUS   Till I shall see you in your soldier's dress,
             Which will become you both, farewell.
MÆCENAS   We shall,
             As I conceive the journey, be at Mount
             Before you, Lepidus.
LEPIDUS   Your way is shorter;
             My purposes do draw me much about:
             You'll win two days upon me.
MÆCENAS, AGRIPPA   Sir, good success!
LEPIDUS   Farewell.   [*Exeunt.* 10

SCENE 5.

Alexandria. Inside Cleopatra's palace.

Enter CLEOPATRA, CHARMIAN, IRAS *and* ALEXAS.

CLEOPATRA Give me some music: music, moody food
          Of us that trade in love.

ALL   The music, ho!

Enter MARDIAN, *the eunuch.*

CLEOPATRA Let it alone; let's to billiards: come, Charmian.

CHARMIAN My arm is sore; best play with Mardian.

CLEOPATRA As well a woman with an eunuch played
          As with a woman. – Come, you'll play with me, sir?

MARDIAN As well as I can, madam.

CLEOPATRA And when good will is showed, though't come
                                                  too short,
          The actor may plead pardon. I'll none now.
          Give me mine angle; we'll to th'river: there,   10
          My music playing far off, I will betray
          Tawny-finned fishes; my bended hook shall pierce
          Their slimy jaws, and, as I draw them up,
          I'll think them every one an Antony,
          And say 'Ah ha! Y'are caught.'

CHARMIAN   'Twas merry when
          You wagered on your angling; when your diver
          Did hang a salt fish on his hook, which he
          With fervency drew up.

CLEOPATRA   That time – O times! –
          I laughed him out of patience; and that night
          I laughed him into patience; and next morn,   20
          Ere the ninth hour, I drunk him to his bed;
          Then put my tires and mantles on him, whilst
          I wore his sword Philippan.[51]

Enter a MESSENGER.

                                  – O, from Italy!
          Ram thou thy fruitful tidings in mine ears,

That long time have been barren.

MESSEN.   Madam, madam —

CLEOPATRA Antonio's dead! If thou say so, villain,
Thou kill'st thy mistress; but well and free,
If thou so yield him, there is gold, and here
My bluest veins to kiss: a hand that kings
Have lipped, and trembled kissing.   30

MESSEN. First, madam, he is well.

CLEOPATRA   Why, there's more gold.
But, sirrah, mark, we use
To say the dead are well: bring it to that,
The gold I give thee will I melt and pour
Down thy ill-uttering throat.

MESSEN. Good madam, hear me.

CLEOPATRA   Well, go to, I will.
But there's no goodness in thy face. If Antony
Be free and healthful, so tart a favour
To trumpet such good tidings? If not well,
Thou shouldst come like a Fury crowned with snakes,   40
Not like a formal man.[52]

MESSEN.   Will't please you hear me?

CLEOPATRA I have a mind to strike thee ere thou speak'st:
Yet, if thou say Antony lives, is well,
Or friends with Cæsar, or not captive to him,
I'll set thee in a shower of gold, and hail
Rich pearls upon thee.

MESSEN.   Madam, he's well.

CLEOPATRA   Well said.

MESSEN. And friends with Cæsar.

CLEOPATRA   Thou'rt an honest man.

MESSEN. Cæsar and he are greater friends than ever.

CLEOPATRA Make thee a fortune from me.

MESSEN.   But yet, madam —

CLEOPATRA I do not like 'But yet': it does allay   50
The good precédence; fie upon 'But yet'!
'But yet' is as a jailor to bring forth
Some monstrous malefactor. Prithee, friend,
Pour out the pack of matter to mine ear,
The good and bad together. He's friends with Cæsar,

In state of health, thou say'st; and, thou say'st, free.

MESSEN.   'Free', madam? No; I made no such report:
He's bound unto Octavia.

CLEOPATRA   For what good turn?

MESSEN.   For the best turn i'th'bed.

CLEOPATRA   I am pale, Charmian.

MESSEN.   Madam, he's married to Octavia.   60

CLEOPATRA The most infectious pestilence upon thee!

                              [*She strikes him down.*

MESSEN.   Good madam, patience.

CLEOPATRA   What say you?
[*She strikes him again.*]   Hence,
Horrible villain, or I'll spurn thine eyes
Like balls before me; I'll unhair thy head!

                         [*She hauls him up and down.*

Thou shalt be whipped with wire, and stewed in brine,
Smarting in ling'ring pickle!

MESSEN.   Gracious madam,
I, that do bring the news, made not the match.

CLEOPATRA Say 'tis not so, a province I will give thee,
And make thy fortunes proud: the blow thou hadst
Shall make thy peace for moving me to rage,   70
And I will boot thee with what gift beside
Thy modesty can beg.

MESSEN.   He's married, madam.

CLEOPATRA Rogue, thou hast lived too long.   [*She draws a knife.*

MESSEN.   Nay, then I'll run.
What mean you, madam? I have made no fault.   [*Exit.*

CHARMIAN Good madam, keep yourself within yourself.
The man is innocent.

CLEOPATRA Some innocents 'scape not the thunderbolt. –
Melt Egypt into Nile, and kindly creatures
Turn all to serpents! – Call the slave again.
Though I am mad, I will not bite him. Call!   80

CHARMIAN He is afeard to come.

CLEOPATRA   I will not hurt him.

                              [*Exit Charmian.*

These hands do lack nobility, that they strike
A meaner than myself; since I myself

Have given myself the cause.

Enter CHARMIAN *with the* MESSENGER.

Come hither, sir.
Though it be honest, it is never good
To bring bad news: give to a gracious message
An host of tongues, but let ill tidings tell
Themselves when they be felt.

MESSEN.   I have done my duty.

CLEOPATRA Is he married?
I cannot hate thee worser than I do,   90
If thou again say 'Yes'.

MESSEN.   He's married, madam.

CLEOPATRA The gods confound thee! Dost thou hold there still?

MESSEN. Should I lie, madam?

CLEOPATRA   O, I would thou didst,
So half my Egypt were submerged and made
A cistern for scaled snakes! Go, get thee hence:
Hadst thou Narcissus in thy face, to me
Thou wouldst appear most ugly. He is married?

MESSEN. I crave your Highness' pardon.

CLEOPATRA   He is married?

MESSEN. Take no offence, that I would not offend you:
To punish me for what you make me do   100
Seems much unequal. He's married to Octavia.

CLEOPATRA O, that his fault should make a knave of thee,
That art not what thou'rt sure of!53 Get thee hence:
The merchandise which thou hast brought from Rome
Are all too dear for me: lie they upon thy hand,
And be undone by 'em!   [*Exit messenger.*

CHARMIAN   Good your Highness, patience.

CLEOPATRA In praising Antony, I have dispraised Cæsar.

CHARMIAN Many times, madam.

CLEOPATRA   I am paid for't now.
Lead me from hence;
I faint, O Iras, Charmian; 'tis no matter.   110
Go to the fellow, good Alexas; bid him
Report the feature of Octavia: her years,
Her inclination; let him not leave out

The colour of her hair. Bring me word quickly.

[*Exit Alexas.*

Let him for ever go! Let him not, Charmian:
Though he be painted one way like a Gorgon,
The other way's a Mars.[54] [*To Mardian:*] Bid you Alexas
Bring me word how tall she is. – Pity me, Charmian,
But do not speak to me. Lead me to my chamber.

[*Exeunt.*

SCENE 6.

Italy. The coast near Misena.

Flourish. Enter, from one side, POMPEY *and* MENAS, *with a* DRUMMER
and a TRUMPETER; *from another,* CÆSAR, ANTONY, LEPIDUS, AGRIPPA,
ENOBARBUS, MÆCENAS *and marching* SOLDIERS. *They halt.*

POMPEY   Your hostages I have, so have you mine;
          And we shall talk before we fight.

CÆSAR   Most meet
          That first we come to words; and therefore have we
          Our written purposes before us sent;
          Which, if thou hast considered, let us know
          If 'twill tie up thy discontented sword
          And carry back to Sicily much tall youth
          That else must perish here.

POMPEY   To you all three,
          The senators alone of this great world,
          Chief factors for the gods: I do not know   10
          Wherefore my father should revengers want,
          Having a son and friends, since Julius Cæsar,
          Who at Philippi the good Brutus ghosted,
          There saw you labouring for him. What was't
          That moved pale Cassius to conspire? And what
          Made the all-honoured honest Roman, Brutus,
          With the armed rest, courtiers of beauteous freedom,
          To drench the Capitol, but that they would
          Have one man but a man?[55] And that is it
          Hath made me rig my navy, at whose burthen   20
          The angered ocean foams; with which I meant

To scourge th'ingratitude that despiteful Rome
Cast on my noble father.[56]

CÆSAR   Take your time.

ANTONY   Thou canst not fear us, Pompey, with thy sails.
We'll speak with thee at sea. At land, thou know'st
How much we do o'ercount thee.

POMPEY   At land, indeed,
Thou dost o'ercount me of my father's house;
But since the cuckoo builds not for himself,
Remain in't as thou mayst.[57]

LEPIDUS   Be pleased to tell us
(For this is from the present) how you take   30
The offers we have sent you.

CÆSAR   There's the point.

ANTONY   Which do not be entreated to, but weigh
What it is worth embraced.

CÆSAR   And what may follow,
To try a larger fortune.

POMPEY   You have made me offer
Of Sicily, Sardinia; and I must
Rid all the sea of pirates; then, to send
Measures of wheat to Rome. This 'greed upon,
To part with unhacked edges and bear back
Our targes undinted.

CÆSAR, ANTONY, LEPIDUS   That's our offer.

POMPEY   Know then,
I came before you here, a man prepared   40
To take this offer. But Mark Antony
Put me to some impatience. Though I lose
The praise of it by telling, you must know,
When Cæsar and your brother were at blows,
Your mother came to Sicily and did find
Her welcome friendly.[58]

ANTONY   I have heard it, Pompey,
And am well studied for a liberal thanks
Which I do owe you.

POMPEY   Let me have your hand.
I did not think, sir, to have met you here.   [*They clasp.*

ANTONY   The beds i'th'East are soft; and thanks to you,   50

| | That called me timelier than my purpose hither, |
| | For I have gained by't. |

CÆSAR   *[to Pompey:]*   Since I saw you last,
There is a change upon you.

POMPEY   Well, I know not
What counts harsh Fortune casts upon my face,
But in my bosom shall she never come,
To make my heart her vassal.

LEPIDUS   Well met here.

POMPEY   I hope so, Lepidus. Thus we are agreed.
I crave our composition may be written
And sealed between us.

CÆSAR   That's the next to do.

POMPEY   We'll feast each other ere we part, and let's   60
Draw lots who shall begin.

ANTONY   That will I, Pompey.

POMPEY   No, Antony, take the lot;
But, first or last, your fine Egyptian cookery
Shall have the fame. I have heard that Julius Cæsar
Grew fat with feasting there.

ANTONY   You have heard much.

POMPEY   I have fair meanings, sir.

ANTONY   And fair words to them.

POMPEY   Then so much have I heard;
And I have heard, Apollodorus carried −

ENOBARB.   No more of that: he did so.

POMPEY   What, I pray you?

ENOBARB.   A certain queen to Cæsar in a mattress.[59]   70

POMPEY   I know thee now. How far'st thou, soldier?

ENOBARB.   Well,
And well am like to do, for I perceive
Four feasts are tóward.

POMPEY   Let me shake thy hand.
I never hated thee: I have seen thee fight,
When I have envied thy behaviour.

ENOBARB.   Sir,
I never loved you much, but I ha'praised ye
When you have well deserved ten times as much
As I have said you did.

POMPEY   Enjoy thy plainness;
It nothing ill becomes thee.
   – Aboard my galley I invite you all: 80
Will you lead, lords?

CÆSAR, ANTONY, LEPIDUS   Show's the way, sir.

POMPEY   Come.

[Exeunt all except Enobarbus and Menas.

MENAS   [*musing:*] Thy father, Pompey, would ne'er have made this treaty. [*To Enobarbus:*] You and I have known, sir.

ENOBARB.   At sea, I think.

MENAS   We have, sir.

ENOBARB.   You have done well by water.

MENAS   And you by land.

ENOBARB.   I will praise any man that will praise me; though it cannot be denied what I have done by land.

MENAS   Nor what I have done by water.   90

ENOBARB.   Yes, something you can deny for your own safety: you have been a great thief by sea.

MENAS   And you by land.

ENOBARB.   There I deny my land service. But give me your hand, Menas: if our eyes had authority, here they might take two thieves kissing.[60]   *[They clasp hands.*

MENAS   All men's faces are true, whatsome'er their hands are.

ENOBARB.   But there is never a fair woman has a true face.

MENAS   No slander; they steal hearts.

ENOBARB.   We came hither to fight with you.   100

MENAS   For my part, I am sorry it is turned to a drinking. Pompey doth this day laugh away his fortune.

ENOBARB.   If he do, sure he cannot weep't back again.

MENAS   Y'have said, sir. We looked not for Mark Antony here: pray you, is he married to Cleopatra?

ENOBARB.   Cæsar's sister is called Octavia.

MENAS   True, sir ; she was the wife of Caius Marcellus.

ENOBARB.   But she is now the wife of Marcus Antonius.

MENAS   Pray ye, sir?

ENOBARB.   'Tis true.   110

MENAS   Then is Cæsar and he for ever knit together.

ENOBARB.   If I were bound to divine of this unity, I would not prophesy so.

MENAS   I think the policy of that purpose made more in the
           marriage than the love of the parties.

ENOBARB.   I think so too. But you shall find, the band that seems to tie
           their friendship together will be the very strangler of their
           amity: Octavia is of a holy, cold, and still conversation.

MENAS   Who would not have his wife so?

ENOBARB.   Not he that himself is not so: which is Mark Antony. 120
           He will to his Egyptian dish again; then shall the sighs of
           Octavia blow the fire up in Cæsar, and, as I said before,
           that which is the strength of their amity shall prove the
           immediate author of their variance. Antony will use his
           affection where it is. He married but his occasion here.

MENAS   And thus it may be. Come, sir, will you aboard? I have a
           health for you.

ENOBARB.   I shall take it, sir: we have used our throats in Egypt.

MENAS   Come, let's away.   [Exeunt.

SCENE 7.

Off Misena. The deck of Pompey's galley.

MUSICIANS *play. Enter two or three* SERVANTS, *setting a dessert.*

SERVANT 1 Here they'll be, man. Some o'their plants are ill-rooted
           already; the least wind i'th'world will blow them down.

SERVANT 2 Lepidus is high-coloured.

SERVANT 1 They have made him drink alms-drink.

SERVANT 2 As they pinch one another by the disposition,[61] he cries
           out 'No more!', reconciles them to his entreaty and
           himself to th'drink.

SERVANT 1 But it raises the greater war between him and his dis-
           cretion.

SERVANT 2 Why, this it is to have a name in great men's fellowship: 10
           I had as lief have a reed that will do me no service as a
           partisan I could not heave.

SERVANT 1 To be called into a huge sphere, and not to be seen to
           move in't, are the holes where eyes should be, which
           pitifully disaster the cheeks.[62]

A sennet is played. Enter CÆSAR, ANTONY, POMPEY, LEPIDUS,
AGRIPPA, MÆCENAS, ENOBARBUS, MENAS, *other*
CAPTAINS *and a* BOY.

ANTONY	[*to Cæsar:*] Thus do they, sir: they take the flow
	o'th'Nile
	By certain scales i'th'pyramid. They know
	By th'height, the lowness, or the mean, if dearth
	Or foison follow. The higher Nilus swells,
	The more it promises: as it ebbs, the seedsman 20
	Upon the slime and ooze scatters his grain,
	And't shortly comes to harvest.
LEPIDUS	Y'have strange serpents there?
ANTONY	Ay, Lepidus.
LEPIDUS	Your serpent of Egypt is bred now of your mud by the
	operation of your sun; so is your crocodile.
ANTONY	They are so.
POMPEY	Sit, and some wine! A health to Lepidus!
LEPIDUS	I am not so well as I should be, but I'll ne'er out.
ENOBARB.	Not till you have slept; I fear me you'll be in till then. 30
LEPIDUS	Nay, certainly, I have heard the Ptolemies' pyramises
	are very goodly things; without contradiction, I have
	heard that.
MENAS	Pompey, a word.
POMPEY	Say in mine ear, what is't?
MENAS	[*whispering:*] Forsake thy seat, I do beseech thee, captain,
	And hear me speak a word.
POMPEY	[*aside to him:*] Forbear me till anon. [*Aloud:*] This wine
	for Lepidus!
LEPIDUS	[*to Antony:*] What manner o'thing is your crocodile?
ANTONY	It is shaped, sir, like itself, and it is as broad as it hath
	breadth. It is just so high as it is, and moves with it own 40
	organs. It lives by that which nourisheth it, and, the
	elements once out of it, it transmigrates.
LEPIDUS	What colour is it of?
ANTONY	Of it own colour too.
LEPIDUS	'Tis a strange serpent.
ANTONY	'Tis so, and the tears of it are wet.
CÆSAR	[*to Antony:*] Will this description satisfy him?

ANTONY   With the health that Pompey gives him, else he is a very
          epicure.   [*Menas whispers again to Pompey.*

POMPEY   [*aside to Menas:*] Go hang, sir, hang! Tell me of that?
                                                          Away! 50
          Do as I bid you. [*Aloud:*] Where's this cup I called for?

MENAS   [*aside to him:*] If for the sake of merit thou wilt hear me,
          Rise from thy stool.

POMPEY   [*aside to Menas:*]   I think thou'rt mad. The matter?
                    [*Pompey rises, and Menas talks privately with him.*

MENAS   I have ever held my cap off to thy fortunes.

POMPEY   Thou hast served me with much faith. What's else to say?
          [*Aloud:*] Be jolly, lords.

ANTONY   These quick-sands, Lepidus,
          Keep off them, for you sink.

MENAS   Wilt thou be lord of all the world?

POMPEY   What say'st thou?

MENAS   Wilt thou be lord of the whole world? That's twice.

POMPEY   How should that be?

MENAS   But entertain it,   60
          And, though thou think me poor, I am the man
          Will give thee all the world.

POMPEY   Hast thou drunk well?

MENAS   No, Pompey, I have kept me from the cup.
          Thou art, if thou dar'st be, the earthly Jove:
          Whate'er the ocean pales, or sky inclips,
          Is thine, if thou wilt ha't.

POMPEY   Show me which way.

MENAS   These three world-sharers, these competitors,
          Are in thy vessel. Let me cut the cable,
          And, when we are put off, fall to their throats.
          All there is thine.

POMPEY   Ah, this thou shouldst have done,   70
          And not have spoke on't! In me 'tis villainy;
          In thee, 't had been good service. Thou must know,
          'Tis not my profit that does lead mine honour;
          Mine honour, it. Repent that e'er thy tongue
          Hath so betrayed thine act. Being done unknown,
          I should have found it afterwards well done,
          But must condemn it now. Desist, and drink.

MENAS   [*to himself:*] For this,
        I'll never follow thy palled fortunes more.
        Who seeks, and will not take when once 'tis offered,   80
        Shall never find it more.
POMPEY   [*having returned:*]   This health to Lepidus!
ANTONY   Bear him ashore. – I'll pledge it for him, Pompey.
ENOBARB. Here's to thee, Menas!
MENAS   Enobarbus, welcome!
POMPEY   Fill till the cup be hid.   [*A servant carries Lepidus away.*
ENOBARB. [*indicating the servant:*] There's a strong fellow, Menas.
MENAS   Why?
ENOBARB. A bears the third part of the world, man; see'st not?
MENAS   The third part then is drunk: would it were all,
        That it might go on wheels!
ENOBARB. Drink thou: increase the reels.   90
MENAS   Come.
POMPEY   This is not yet an Alexandrian feast.
ANTONY   It ripens towards it. – Strike the vessels, ho!
        Here's to Cæsar!
CÆSAR   I could well forbear't:
        It's monstrous labour, when I wash my brain
        And it grows fouler.
ANTONY   Be a child o'th'time.
CÆSAR   'Possess it', I'll make answer;[63]
        But I had rather fast from all, four days,
        Than drink so much in one.
ENOBARB. [*to Antony:*]   Ha, my brave Emperor!
        Shall we dance now the Egyptian Bacchanals,   100
        And celebrate our drink?
POMPEY   Let's ha't, good soldier.
ANTONY   Come, let's all take hands,
        Till that the conquering wine hath steeped our sense
        In soft and delicate Lethe.
ENOBARB.   All take hands.
        – Make battery to our ears with the loud music! –
        The while, I'll place you; then the boy shall sing.
        The holding every man shall bear as loud
        As his strong sides can volley.
            [*Music plays. Enobarbus places them hand in hand.*

BOY *sings (as the carousers dance):*

> Come, thou monarch of the vine,
> Plumpy Bacchus with pink eyne: 110
> In thy fats our cares be drowned;
> With thy grapes our hairs be crowned.

BOY *and* OTHERS

> Cup us, till the world go round;
> Cup us, till the world go round!

CÆSAR   What would you more? Pompey, good night.
                    [*To Antony:*] Good brother,
Let me request you off: our graver business
Frowns at this levity. – Gentle lords, let's part;
You see we have burnt our cheeks. Strong Enobarb
Is weaker than the wine, and mine own tongue
Spleets what it speaks: the wild disguise hath almost   120
Anticked us all. What needs more words? Good night.
– Good Antony, your hand.

POMPEY   I'll try you on the shore.

ANTONY   And shall, sir; give's your hand.

POMPEY   O Antony,
You have my father's house. But what? We are friends.
Come down into the boat.

ENOBARB.   Take heed you fall not.
          [*Exeunt all except Enobarbus, Menas and the musicians.*
Menas, I'll not on shore.

MENAS   No, to my cabin.
          [*To musicians:*] These drums, these trumpets, flutes: what?
Let Neptune hear we bid a loud farewell
To these great fellows: sound and be hanged, sound out!
                    [*The musicians sound a flourish, with drums.*

ENOBARB.   'Hoo!' says a. There's my cap.   130
                    [*He throws it into the air.*

MENAS   Hoo! Noble captain, come.   [*Exeunt.*

ACT 3, SCENE 1.

Somewhere in the Middle East.

Enter VENTIDIUS *in triumph (the corpse of* PACORUS *borne before him),*
SILLIUS *and other Roman* SOLDIERS.

VENTID. Now, darting Parthia, art thou struck, and now
Pleased Fortune does of Marcus Crassus' death
Make me revenger. Bear the King's son's body
Before our army. Thy Pacorus, Orodes,
Pays this for Marcus Crassus.⁶⁴

SILLIUS   Noble Ventidius,
Whilst yet with Parthian blood thy sword is warm,
The fugitive Parthians follow. Spur through Media,
Mesopotamia, and the shelters whither
The routed fly. So thy grand captain, Antony,
Shall set thee on triumphant chariots and
Put garlands on thy head.

VENTID.   O Sillius, Silllius,
I have done enough. A lower place, note well,
May make too great an act. For learn this, Sillius:
Better to leave undone, than by our deed
Acquire too high a fame, when him we serve's away.
Cæsar and Antony have ever won
More in their officer than person. Sossius,
One of my place in Syria, his lieutenant,
For quick accumulation of renown,
Which he achieved by th'minute, lost his favour.
Who does i'th'wars more than his captain can
Becomes his captain's captain; and ambition
(The soldier's virtue) rather makes choice of loss
Than gain which darkens him.
I could do more to do Antonius good,
But 'twould offend him; and in his offence
Should my performance perish.

SILLIUS Thou hast, Ventidius, that
Without the which a soldier and his sword

10

20

	Grants scarce distinction.[65] Thou wilt write to Antony? 30
VENTID.	I'll humbly signify what in his name,
	That magical word of war, we have effected;
	How, with his banners and his well-paid ranks,
	The ne'er-yet-beaten horse of Parthia
	We have jaded out o'th'field.
SILLIUS	Where is he now?
VENTID.	He purposeth to Athens: whither, with what haste
	The weight we must convey with's will permit,
	We shall appear before him. – On, there; pass along!
	[*Exeunt.*

SCENE 2.

Rome.

Enter AGRIPPA *at one door,* ENOBARBUS *at another.*

AGRIPPA	What, are the brothers parted?
ENOBARB.	They have dispatched with Pompey; he is gone;
	The other three are sealing. Octavia weeps
	To part from Rome; Cæsar is sad; and Lepidus,
	Since Pompey's feast, as Menas says, is troubled
	With the green sickness.
AGRIPPA	'Tis a noble Lepidus.
ENOBARB.	A very fine one: O, how he loves Cæsar!
AGRIPPA	Nay, but how dearly he adores Mark Antony!
ENOBARB.	Cæsar? Why, he's the Jupiter of men.
AGRIPPA	What's Antony: the god of Jupiter?
ENOBARB.	Spake you of Cæsar? How, the nonpareil? 10
AGRIPPA	O Antony, O thou Arabian bird!
ENOBARB.	Would you praise Cæsar, say 'Cæsar': go no further.
AGRIPPA	Indeed, he plied them both with excellent praises.
ENOBARB.	But he loves Cæsar best; yet he loves Antony.
	Hoo! Hearts, tongues, figures, scribes, bards,
	poets, cannot
	Think, speak, cast, write, sing, number – hoo! –
	His love to Antony. But as for Cæsar,
	Kneel down, kneel down, and wonder.
AGRIPPA	Both he loves.

ENOBARB. They are his shards, and he their beetle.[66]
          [*Trumpets are heard.*]   So!   20
          This is to horse. Adieu, noble Agrippa.
AGRIPPA   Good fortune, worthy soldier, and farewell.

          Enter CÆSAR, ANTONY, LEPIDUS *and* OCTAVIA.

ANTONY   [*to Cæsar:*] No further, sir.
CÆSAR   You take from me a great part of myself;
          Use me well in't. — Sister, prove such a wife
          As my thoughts make thee, and as my farthest band
          Shall pass on thy approof.[67] — Most noble Antony,
          Let not the piece of virtue which is set
          Betwixt us as the cément of our love,
          To keep it builded, be the ram to batter   30
          The fortress of it; for better might we
          Have loved without this mean, if on both parts
          This be not cherished.
ANTONY   Make me not offended
          In your distrust.
CÆSAR   I have said.
ANTONY   You shall not find,
          Though you be therein curious, the least cause
          For what you seem to fear; so, the gods keep you,
          And make the hearts of Romans serve your ends!
          We will here part.
CÆSAR   — Farewell, my dearest sister, fare thee well.
          The elements be kind to thee, and make
          Thy spirits all of comfort! Fare thee well.   40
OCTAVIA   My noble brother!   [*She weeps.*
ANTONY   The April's in her eyes: it is love's spring,
          And these the showers to bring it on. — Be cheerful.
OCTAVIA   [*to Cæsar:*] Sir, look well to my husband's house, and —
CÆSAR   What,
          Octavia?
OCTAVIA   I'll tell you in your ear.   [*She whispers to him.*
ANTONY   Her tongue will not obey her heart, nor can
          Her heart inform her tongue: the swan's-down feather,
          That stands upon the swell at full of tide
          And neither way inclines.   50

ENOBARB. [to Agrippa:] Will Cæsar weep?

AGRIPPA   He has a cloud in's face.

ENOBARB. He were the worse for that, were he a horse;[68]
    So is he, being a man.

AGRIPPA   Why, Enobarbus,
    When Antony found Julius Cæsar dead,
    He cried almost to roaring; and he wept
    When at Philippi he found Brutus slain.

ENOBARB. That year, indeed, he was troubled with a rheum;
    What willingly he did confound, he wailed,
    Believe't, till I wept too.[69]

CÆSAR   No, sweet Octavia,
    You shall hear from me still; the time shall not   60
    Out-go my thinking on you.

ANTONY   Come, sir, come;
    I'll wrestle with you in my strength of love:
    Look, here I have you [hugging him]; thus I let you go,
    And give you to the gods.

CÆSAR   Adieu; be happy.

LEPIDUS Let all the number of the stars give light
    To thy fair way!

CÆSAR   Farewell, farewell! [He kisses Octavia.

ANTONY   Farewell!
    [Trumpets sound. Exeunt as two separate groups.

SCENE 3.

Alexandria. Inside Cleopatra's palace.

Enter CLEOPATRA, CHARMIAN, IRAS *and* ALEXAS.

CLEOPATRA Where is the fellow?

ALEXAS   Half afeard to come.

CLEOPATRA Go to, go to.

    Enter the MESSENGER *again.*

    – Come hither, sir.

ALEXAS   Good Majesty,
    Herod of Jewry dare not look upon you
    But when you are well pleased.

CLEOPATRA   That Herod's head

	I'll have;[70] but how, when Antony is gone,	
	Through whom I might command it? – Come thou near.	
MESSEN.	Most gracious Majesty.	
CLEOPATRA	Didst thou behold	
	Octavia?	
MESSEN.	Ay, dread Queen.	
CLEOPATRA	Where?	
MESSEN.	Madam, in Rome:	
	I looked her in the face, and saw her led	
	Between her brother and Mark Antony.	10

CLEOPATRA Is she as tall as me?

MESSEN.   She is not, madam.

CLEOPATRA Didst hear her speak? Is she shrill-tongued or low?

MESSEN.   Madam, I heard her speak; she is low-voiced.

CLEOPATRA That's not so good: he cannot like her long.

CHARMIAN 'Like her'? O Isis! 'Tis impossible.

CLEOPATRA I think so, Charmian: dull of tongue, and dwarfish.
What majesty is in her gait? Remember,
If e'er thou look'st on majesty.

MESSEN.   She creeps:
Her motion and her station are as one;
She shows a body rather than a life,   20
A statue than a breather.

CLEOPATRA   Is this certain?

MESSEN.   Or I have no observance.

CHARMIAN   Three in Egypt
Cannot make better note.

CLEOPATRA   He's very knowing;
I do perceive't: there's nothing in her yet.
The fellow has good judgement.

CHARMIAN   Excellent.

CLEOPATRA Guess at her years, I prithee.

MESSEN.   Madam,
She was a widow –

CLEOPATRA   'Widow'? Charmian, hark.

MESSEN.   And I do think she's thirty.[71]

CLEOPATRA Bear'st thou her face in mind? Is't long or round?

MESSEN.   Round, even to faultiness.   30

CLEOPATRA For the most part, too, they are foolish that are so.

        Her hair, what colour?

MESSEN.   Brown, madam; and her forehead
        As low as she would wish it.

CLEOPATRA   There's gold for thee.
        Thou must not take my former sharpness ill;
        I will employ thee back again: I find thee
        Most fit for business. Go, make thee ready;
        Our letters are prepared.   [*Exit messenger.*

CHARMIAN   A proper man.

CLEOPATRA Indeed, he is so: I repent me much
        That so I harried him. Why, methinks, by him,
        This creature's no such thing.

CHARMIAN   Nothing, madam.   40

CLEOPATRA The man hath seen some majesty, and should know.

CHARMIAN Hath he seen majesty? Isis else defend,
        And serving you so long!

CLEOPATRA I have one thing more to ask him yet, good Charmian.
        But 'tis no matter; thou shalt bring him to me
        Where I will write. All may be well enough.

CHARMIAN I warrant you, madam.   [*Exeunt.*

SCENE 4.

Athens. Inside Antony's house.

Enter ANTONY *and* OCTAVIA.

ANTONY   Nay, nay, Octavia, not only that
        (That were excusable, that and thousands more
        Of semblable import), but he hath waged
        New wars 'gainst Pompey; made his will, and read it
        To public ear;
        Spoke scantly of me; when perforce he could not
        But pay me terms of honour, cold and sickly
        He vented them, most narrow measure lent me;
        When the best hint was given him, he not took't,
        Or did it from his teeth.

OCTAVIA   O my good lord,   10
        Believe not all, or, if you must believe,
        Stomach not all. A more unhappy lady,

If this division chance, ne'er stood between,
Praying for both parts:
The good gods will mock me presently,
When I shall pray, 'O, bless my lord and husband!',
Undo that prayer, by crying out as loud,
'O, bless my brother!'. Husband win, win brother,
Prays, and destroys the prayer: no midway
'Twixt these extremes at all.

ANTONY   Gentle Octavia,   20
Let your best love draw to that point which seeks
Best to preserve it: if I lose mine honour,
I lose myself: better I were not yours,
Than yours so branchless. But, as you requested,
Yourself shall go between's; the meantime, lady,
I'll raise the preparation of a war
Shall stain your brother. Make your soonest haste;
So your desires are yours.

OCTAVIA   Thanks to my lord.
The Jove of power make me, most weak, most weak,
Your reconciler! Wars 'twixt you twain would be   30
As if the world should cleave, and that slain men
Should solder up the rift.

ANTONY   When it appears to you where this begins,
Turn your displeasure that way; for our faults
Can never be so equal, that your love
Can equally move with them. Provide your going;
Choose your own company, and command what cost
Your heart has mind to.   [*Exeunt separately.*

SCENE 5.

Athens. Inside Antony's house.

Enter ENOBARBUS *and* EROS, *meeting.*

ENOBARB. How now, friend Eros?

EROS   There's strange news come, sir.

ENOBARB. What, man?

EROS   Cæsar and Lepidus have made wars upon Pompey.

ENOBARB. This is old; what is the success?

EROS   Cæsar, having made use of him in the wars 'gainst
          Pompey, presently denied him rivality, would not let
          him partake in the glory of the action, and, not resting
          here, accuses him of letters he had formerly wrote to
          Pompey; upon his own appeal, seizes him: so the poor   10
          third is up, till death enlarge his confine.

ENOBARB. Then, world, thou hast a pair of chaps, no more;
          And throw between them all the food thou hast,
          They'll grind the one the other. Where's Antony?

EROS   He's walking in the garden, thus, and spurns
          The rush that lies before him; cries 'Fool Lepidus!',
          And threats the throat of that his officer
          That murdered Pompey.[72]

ENOBARB.   Our great navy's rigged.

EROS   For Italy and Cæsar. More, Domitius:
          My lord desires you presently; my news   20
          I might have told hereafter.

ENOBARB.   'Twill be naught:
          But let it be. Bring me to Antony.

EROS   Come, sir.   [*Exeunt.*

SCENE 6.

Rome. Inside Cæsar's house.

Enter CÆSAR, AGRIPPA *and* MÆCENAS.

CÆSAR Contemning Rome, he has done all this and more
In Alexandria. Here's the manner of't:
I'th'market-place, on a tribunal silvered,
Cleopatra and himself in chairs of gold
Were publicly enthroned; at the feet sat
Cæsarion, whom they call my father's son,
And all the unlawful issue that their lust
Since then hath made between them.[73] Unto her
He gave the stablishment of Egypt; made her
Of lower Syria, Cyprus, Lydia,   10
Absolute Queen.

MÆCENAS   This in the public eye?

CÆSAR I'th'common show-place, where they exercise.
His sons he there proclaimed the kings of kings:
Great Media, Parthia and Armenia
He gave to Alexander; to Ptolemy he assigned
Syria, Cilicia and Phœnicia. She
In th'habiliments of the goddess Isis
That day appeared, and oft before gave audience,
As 'tis reported, so.

MÆCENAS   Let Rome be thus
Informed.

AGRIPPA   Who, queasy with his insolence   20
Already, will their good thoughts call from him.

CÆSAR The people know it, and have now received
His accusations.

AGRIPPA   Who does he accuse?

CÆSAR Cæsar; and that having in Sicily
Sextus Pompeius spoiled, we had not rated him
His part o'th'isle. Then does he say, he lent me
Some shipping unrestored. Lastly, he frets
That Lepidus of the Triumvirate
Should be deposed; and, being, that we detain

All his revénue.

AGRIPPA   Sir, this should be answered.   30

CÆSAR 'Tis done already, and the messenger gone.
I have told him, Lepidus was grown too cruel,
That he his high authority abused,
And did deserve his change. For what I have conquered,
I grant him part; but then, in his Armenia
And other of his conquered kingdoms, I
Demand the like.

MÆCENAS   He'll never yield to that.

CÆSAR Nor must not then be yielded to in this.

Enter OCTAVIA, *with two or three* ATTENDANTS.

OCTAVIA Hail, Cæsar, and my lord! Hail, most dear Cæsar!

CÆSAR That ever I should call thee castaway!   40

OCTAVIA You have not called me so, nor have you cause.

CÆSAR Why have you stol'n upon us thus? You come not
Like Cæsar's sister. The wife of Antony
Should have an army for an usher, and
The neighs of horse to tell of her approach
Long ere she did appear. The trees by th'way
Should have borne men, and expectation fainted,
Longing for what it had not. Nay, the dust
Should have ascended to the roof of heaven,
Raised by your populous troops. But you are come   50
A market-maid to Rome, and have prevented
The ostentation of our love, which, left unshown,
Is often left unloved.[74] We should have met you
By sea and land, supplying every stage
With an augmented greeting.

OCTAVIA   Good my lord,
To come thus was I not constrained, but did it
On my free will. My lord, Mark Antony,
Hearing that you prepared for war, acquainted
My grievèd ear withal; whereon I begged
His pardon for return.

CÆSAR   Which soon he granted,   60
Being an abstract 'tween his lust and him.[75]

OCTAVIA Do not say so, my lord.

CÆSAR   I have eyes upon him,

And his affairs come to me on the wind.
Where is he now?
OCTAVIA   My lord, in Athens.
CÆSAR   No, my most wrongèd sister: Cleopatra
Hath nodded him to her. He hath given his empire
Up to a whore, who now are levying
The kings o'th'earth for war. He hath assembled
Bocchus, the King of Libya; Archelaus
Of Cappadocia; Philadelphos, King   70
Of Paphlagonia; the Thracian King, Adallas;
King Manchus of Arabia; King of Pont;
Herod of Jewry; Mithridates, King
Of Comagene; Polemon and Amyntas,
The Kings of Mede and Lycaonia;
With a more larger list of sceptres.
OCTAVIA   Ay me, most wretched,
That have my heart parted betwixt two friends
That does afflict each other!
CÆSAR   Welcome hither.
Your letters did withhold our breaking forth,
Till we perceived both how you were wrong led   80
And we in negligent danger. Cheer your heart:
Be you not troubled with the time, which drives
O'er your content these strong necessities,
But let determined things to destiny
Hold unbewailed their way. Welcome to Rome;
Nothing more dear to me. You are abused
Beyond the mark of thought; and the high gods,
To do you justice, makes his ministers
Of us and those that love you.[76] Best of comfort,
And ever welcome to us.
AGRIPPA   Welcome, lady.   90
MÆCENAS Welcome, dear madam.
Each heart in Rome does love and pity you.
Only th'adulterous Antony, most large
In his abominations, turns you off,
And gives his potent regiment to a trull
That noises it against us.[77]
OCTAVIA   Is it so, sir?

CÆSAR   Most certain. Sister, welcome: pray you,
          Be ever known to patience. My dear'st sister!   [*Exeunt.*

SCENE 7.

Antony's headquarters near Actium in Greece.

Enter CLEOPATRA *and* ENOBARBUS.

CLEOPATRA I will be even with thee, doubt it not.
ENOBARB. But why, why, why?
CLEOPATRA Thou hast forspoke my being in these wars,
          And say'st it is not fit.
ENOBARB.   Well: is it, is it?
CLEOPATRA Is't not denounced against us? Why should not we
          Be there in person? [78]
ENOBARB. [*to himself:*]   Well, I could reply:
          If we should serve with horse and mares together,
          The horse were merely lost; the mares would bear
          A soldier and his horse.
CLEOPATRA   What is't you say?
ENOBARB. Your presence needs must puzzle Antony,   10
          Take from his heart, take from his brain, from's time,
          What should not then be spared. He is already
          Traduced for levity, and 'tis said in Rome
          That Photinus, an eunuch, and your maids
          Manage this war.
CLEOPATRA   Sink Rome, and their tongues rot
          That speak against us! A charge we bear i'th'war,
          And, as the president of my kingdom, will
          Appear there for a man. Speak not against it,
          I will not stay behind.

Enter ANTONY *and* CANIDIUS.

ENOBARB.   Nay, I have done.
          Here comes the Emperor.
ANTONY   Is it not strange, Canidius,   20
          That from Tarentum and Brundusium
          He could so quickly cut the Ionian sea,
          And take in Toryne? You have heard on't, sweet?

CLEOPATRA Celerity is never more admired
          Than by the negligent.
ANTONY   A good rebuke,
          Which might have well becomed the best of men,
          To taunt at slackness. Canidius, we
          Will fight with him by sea.
CLEOPATRA   By sea: what else?
CANIDIUS Why will my lord do so?
ANTONY   For that he dares us to't.
ENOBARB. So hath my lord dared him to single fight.   30
CANIDIUS Ay, and to wage this battle at Pharsalia,
          Where Cæsar fought with Pompey. But these offers,
          Which serve not for his vantage, he shakes off;
          And so should you.
ENOBARB.   Your ships are not well manned,
          Your mariners are muleters, reapers, people
          Ingrossed by swift impress. In Cæsar's fleet
          Are those that often have 'gainst Pompey fought.
          Their ships are yare, yours heavy. No disgrace
          Shall fall you for refusing him at sea,
          Being prepared for land.
ANTONY   By sea, by sea.   40
ENOBARB. Most worthy sir, you therein throw away
          The absolute soldiership you have by land;
          Distract your army, which doth most consist
          Of war-marked footmen; leave unexecuted
          Your own renownèd knowledge; quite forgo
          The way which promises assurance; and
          Give up yourself merely to chance and hazard
          From firm security.
ANTONY   I'll fight at sea.
CLEOPATRA I have sixty sails, Cæsar none better.
ANTONY   Our overplus of shipping will we burn,   50
          And, with the rest full-manned, from th'head of Actium
          Beat th'approaching Cæsar. But if we fail,
          We then can do't at land.

                    Enter a MESSENGER.

                              – Thy business?

MESSEN.	The news is true, my lord: he is descried.
	Cæsar has taken Toryne.
ANTONY	Can he be there in person? 'Tis impossible.
	Strange that his power should be. Canidius,
	Our nineteen legions thou shalt hold by land,
	And our twelve thousand horse. We'll to our ship.
	– Away, my Thetis![79]

Enter a SOLDIER.

– How now, worthy soldier?   60

SOLDIER	O noble Emperor, do not fight by sea;
	Trust not to rotten planks. Do you misdoubt
	This sword and these my wounds? Let th'Egyptians
	And the Phœnicians go a-ducking; we
	Have used to conquer standing on the earth
	And fighting foot to foot.
ANTONY	Well, well, away!

[*Exeunt Antony, Cleopatra and Enobarbus.*

SOLDIER	By Hercules, I think I am i'th'right.
CANIDIUS	Soldier, thou art; but his whole action grows
	Not in the power on't:[80] so our leader's led,
	And we are women's men.
SOLDIER	You keep by land 70
	The legions and the horse whole, do you not?
CANIDIUS	Marcus Octavius, Marcus Justeius,
	Publicola and Cælius are for sea;
	But we keep whole by land. This speed of Cæsar's
	Carries beyond belief.
SOLDIER	While he was yet in Rome,
	His power went out in such distractions as
	Beguiled all spies.
CANIDIUS	Who's his lieutenant, hear you?
SOLDIER	They say, one Taurus.
CANIDIUS	Well, I know the man.

Enter a MESSENGER.

MESSEN.	The Emperor calls Canidius.
CANIDIUS	With news the time's in labour, and throws forth
	Each minute some.[81] [*Exeunt.* 8

SCENE 8.

Near Actium.

Enter CÆSAR *and* TAURUS, *with Cæsar's marching* ARMY.

CÆSAR   Taurus!
TAURUS   My lord?
CÆSAR   Strike not by land; keep whole; provoke not battle
           Till we have done at sea. Do not exceed
           The prescript of this scroll: our fortune lies
           Upon this jump.   [*He gives the scroll to Taurus. Exeunt.*

SCENE 9.

Near Actium.

Enter ANTONY *and* ENOBARBUS.

ANTONY   Set we our squadrons on yond side o'th'hill,
           In eye of Cæsar's battle; from which place
           We may the number of the ships behold,
           And so proceed accordingly.   [*Exeunt.*

SCENE 10.

Near Actium.

Enter CANIDIUS *and his* ARMY, *marching. Exeunt.*
Enter TAURUS *and his* ARMY, *marching the other way. Exeunt.*
The noise of a sea-battle is heard.

Alarum. Enter ENOBARBUS.

ENOBARB.   Naught, naught, all naught! I can behold no longer:
           Th'*Antoniad*, the Egyptian admiral,
           With all their sixty, fly and turn the rudder:
           To see't, mine eyes are blasted.

Enter SCARRUS.

SCARRUS   Gods and goddesses,
           All the whole synod of them!
ENOBARB.   What's thy passion?

SCARRUS   The greater cantle of the world is lost
            With very ignorance. We have kissed away
            Kingdoms and provinces.

ENOBARB.   How appears the fight?

SCARRUS   On our side like the tokened pestilence,
            Where death is sure. Yon ribaudred nag of Egypt[82]   10
            (Whom leprosy o'ertake), i'th'midst o'th'fight,
            When vantage like a pair of twins appeared,
            Both as the same, or rather ours the elder,
            The breeze upon her, like a cow in June,
            Hoists sails and flies.

ENOBARB.   That I beheld:
            Mine eyes did sicken at the sight, and could not
            Endure a further view.

SCARRUS   She once being loofed,
            The noble ruin of her magic, Antony,
            Claps on his sea-wing, and (like a doting mallard),   20
            Leaving the fight in height, flies after her.
            I never saw an action of such shame:
            Experience, manhood, honour, ne'er before
            Did violate so itself.

ENOBARB.   Alack, alack!

Enter CANIDIUS.

CANIDIUS   Our fortune on the sea is out of breath,
            And sinks most lamentably. Had our General
            Been what he knew himself, it had gone well.
            O, he has given example for our flight
            Most grossly by his own!

ENOBARB.   Ay, are you thereabouts?   30
            Why then good night indeed.

CANIDIUS   Toward Peloponnesus are they fled.

SCARRUS   'Tis easy to't; and there I will attend
            What further comes.

CANIDIUS   To Cæsar will I render
            My legions and my horse. Six kings already
            Show me the way of yielding.

ENOBARB.   I'll yet follow
            The wounded chance of Antony, though my reason
            Sits in the wind against me.   [*Exeunt.*

SCENE 11.

Alexandria.

Enter ANTONY *and* ATTENDANTS.

ANTONY Hark: the land bids me tread no more upon't;
It is ashamed to bear me. Friends, come hither.
I am so lated in the world that I
Have lost my way for ever. I have a ship
Laden with gold; take that, divide it; fly,
And make your peace with Cæsar.

ATTENDANTS   Fly? Not we.

ANTONY I have fled myself, and have instructed cowards
To run and show their shoulders. Friends, be gone;
I have myself resolved upon a course
Which has no need of you. Be gone.   10
My treasure's in the harbour. Take it. O,
I followed that I blush to look upon!
My very hairs do mutiny, for the white
Reprove the brown for rashness, and they them
For fear and doting. Friends, be gone; you shall
Have letters from me to some friends that will
Sweep your way for you. Pray you, look not sad,
Nor make replies of loathness; take the hint
Which my despair proclaims. Let that be left
Which leaves itself. To the sea-side straightway: 20
I will possess you of that ship and treasure.
Leave me, I pray, a little; pray you now.
Nay, do so; for indeed I have lost command:
Therefore I pray you. I'll see you by and by.

                    [*Exeunt attendants. Antony sits.*

Enter CLEOPATRA, *led by* CHARMIAN, IRAS *and* EROS.

EROS   Nay, gentle madam: to him, comfort him.
IRAS   Do, most dear Queen.
CHARMIAN Do; why, what else?
CLEOPATRA Let me sit down. O Juno!   [*She sits.*
ANTONY No, no, no, no, no.

EROS	See you here, sir?	30
ANTONY	O fie, fie, fie!	
CHARMIAN	Madam.	
IRAS	Madam, O good Empress!	
EROS	Sir, sir!	

ANTONY   Yes, my lord, yes. [*Musing:*] He at Philippi kept
His sword e'en like a dancer, while I struck
The lean and wrinkled Cassius; and 'twas I
That the mad Brutus ended. He alone
Dealt on lieutenantry and no practice had
In the brave squares of war.[83] Yet now – no matter.   40

CLEOPATRA Ah; stand by.

EROS   The Queen, my lord, the Queen.

IRAS   Go to him, madam, speak to him:
He is unqualitied with very shame.

CLEOPATRA Well then, sustain me; O! [*Supported, she approaches him.*]

EROS   Most noble sir, arise, the Queen approaches.
Her head's declined, and death will seize her, but
Your comfort makes the rescue.

ANTONY   I have offended reputation,
A most unnoble swerving.

EROS   Sir, the Queen.   50

ANTONY   O, whither hast thou led me, Egypt? See
How I convey my shame out of thine eyes,
By looking back what I have left behind
'Stroyed in dishonour.

CLEOPATRA   O my lord, my lord,
Forgive my fearful sails! I little thought
You would have followed.

ANTONY   Egypt, thou knew'st too well
My heart was to thy rudder tied by th'strings,
And thou shouldst tow me after. O'er my spirit
Thy full supremacy thou knew'st, and that
Thy beck might from the bidding of the gods   60
Command me.

CLEOPATRA   O, my pardon!

ANTONY   Now I must
To the young man send humble treaties, dodge
And palter in the shifts of lowness, who

With half the bulk o'th'world played as I pleased,
Making and marring fortunes. You did know
How much you were my conqueror, and that
My sword, made weak by my affection, would
Obey it on all cause.

CLEOPATRA   Pardon, pardon!

ANTONY   Fall not a tear, I say; one of them rates
All that is won and lost. Give me a kiss.   [*They kiss.* 70
Even this repays me.
We sent our schoolmaster;[84] is a come back?
Love, I am full of lead. [*He calls:*] Some wine,
Within there, and our viands! – Fortune knows,
We scorn her most when most she offers blows. [*Exeunt.*

SCENE 12.

Egypt. Cæsar's camp.

Enter CÆSAR, AGRIPPA, DOLABELLA, THIDIAS *and* OTHERS.

CÆSAR   Let him appear that's come from Antony.
Know you him?

DOLABELL.   Cæsar, 'tis his schoolmaster:
An argument that he is plucked, when hither
He sends so poor a pinion of his wing,
Which had superfluous kings for messengers
Not many moons gone by.

Enter Antony's AMBASSADOR *(the schoolmaster).*

CÆSAR   Approach, and speak.

AMBASS.   Such as I am, I come from Antony.
I was of late as petty to his ends
As is the morn-dew on the myrtle-leaf
To his grand sea.

CÆSAR   Be't so: declare thine office.   10

AMBASS.   Lord of his fortunes he salutes thee, and
Requires to live in Egypt; which not granted,
He lessens his requests, and to thee sues
To let him breathe between the heavens and earth,
A private man in Athens: this for him.

Next, Cleopatra does confess thy greatness,
Submits her to thy might, and of thee craves
The circle of the Ptolemies for her heirs,
Now hazarded to thy grace.

CÆSAR   For Antony,
I have no ears to his request. The Queen   20
Of audience nor desire shall fail, so she
From Egypt drive her all-disgracèd friend,
Or take his life there. This if she perform,
She shall not sue unheard. So to them both.

AMBASS.   Fortune pursue thee.

CÆSAR   – Bring him through the bands.
                    [Exit ambassador, attended.
[To Thidias:] To try thy eloquence now 'tis time:
                              dispatch;

From Antony win Cleopatra: promise,
And in our name, what she requires; add more
(From thine invention) offers. Women are not
In their best fortunes strong, but want will perjure   30
The ne'er-touched vestal. Try thy cunning, Thidias;
Make thine own edict for thy pains, which we
Will answer as a law.[85]

THIDIAS   Cæsar, I go.

CÆSAR   Observe how Antony becomes his flaw,
And what thou think'st his very action speaks
In every power that moves.

THIDIAS   Cæsar, I shall.   [Exeunt.

SCENE 13.

Alexandria. Inside Cleopatra's palace.

Enter CLEOPATRA, ENOBARBUS, CHARMIAN *and* IRAS.

CLEOPATRA What shall we do, Enobarbus?
ENOBARB.   Think, and die.
CLEOPATRA Is Antony or we in fault for this?
ENOBARB. Antony only, that would make his will
          Lord of his reason. What though you fled

From that great face of war, whose several ranges
Frighted each other? Why should he follow?
The itch of his affection should not then
Have nicked his captainship at such a point,
When half to half the world opposed, he being
The meréd question. 'Twas a shame no less   10
Than was his loss, to course your flying flags
And leave his navy gazing.

CLEOPATRA   Prithee, peace.

Enter ANTONY *with the* AMBASSADOR.

ANTONY   Is that his answer?
AMBASS.   Ay, my lord.
ANTONY   The Queen shall then have courtesy, so she
Will yield us up.
AMBASS.   He says so.
ANTONY   Let her know't.
[*To Cleopatra:*] To the boy Cæsar send this grizzled head,
And he will fill thy wishes to the brim
With principalities.
CLEOPATRA   That head, my lord?
ANTONY   [*to ambassador:*] To him again! Tell him he wears the rose   20
Of youth upon him; from which the world should note
Something particular: his coin, ships, legions,
May be a coward's, whose ministers would prevail
Under the service of a child as soon
As i'th'command of Cæsar. I dare him therefore
To lay his gay comparison apart[86]
And answer me declined, sword against sword,
Ourselves alone. I'll write it: follow me.

                          [*Exeunt Antony and ambassador.*

ENOBARB.   Yes, like enough: high-battled Cæsar will
Unstate his happiness, and be staged to th'show   30
Against a sworder! I see men's judgements are
A parcel of their fortunes, and things outward
Do draw the inward quality after them,
To suffer all alike. That he should dream,
Knowing all measures, the full Cæsar will
Answer his emptiness! Cæsar, thou hast subdued
His judgement too.

Enter a SERVANT.

SERVANT	A messenger from Cæsar.
CLEOPATRA	What, no more ceremony? – See, my women,

Against the blown rose may they stop their nose,
That kneeled unto the buds. – Admit him, sir.   40

[*Exit servant.*

ENOBARB. [*to himself:*] Mine honesty and I begin to square.
The loyalty well held to fools does make
Our faith mere folly; yet he that can endure
To follow with allegiance a fall'n lord
Does conquer him that did his master conquer,
And earns a place i'th'story.

Enter THIDIAS.

CLEOPATRA	Cæsar's will?
THIDIAS	Hear it apart.
CLEOPATRA	None but friends: say boldly.
THIDIAS	So, haply, are they friends to Antony.
ENOBARB.	He needs as many, sir, as Cæsar has,

Or needs not us. If Cæsar please, our master   50
Will leap to be his friend. For us, you know,
Whose he is we are, and that is Cæsar's.

THIDIAS	So. –

Thus then, thou most renowned, Cæsar entreats
Not to consider in what case thou stand'st
Further than he is Cæsar.[87]

CLEOPATRA	Go on; right royal.
THIDIAS	He knows that you embraced not Antony

As you did love, but as you feared him.

CLEOPATRA	O.
THIDIAS	The scars upon your honour, therefore, he

Does pity as constrainèd blemishes,
Not as deserved.

CLEOPATRA	He is a god, and knows 60

What is most right. Mine honour was not yielded,
But conquered merely.

ENOBARB. [*to himself:*]   To be sure of that,
I will ask Antony. [*He muses:*] Sir, sir, thou art so leaky
That we must leave thee to thy sinking, for

| | Thy dearest quit thee. | [*Exit.* |

THIDIAS   Shall I say to Cæsar
What you require of him? For he partly begs
To be desired to give. It much would please him,
That of his fortunes you should make a staff
To lean upon. But it would warm his spirits
To hear from me you had left Antony,   70
And put yourself under his shroud,
The universal landlord.
CLEOPATRA   What's your name?
THIDIAS   My name is Thidias.
CLEOPATRA   Most kind messenger,
Say to great Cæsar this in deputation:
I kiss his conqu'ring hand. Tell him, I am prompt
To lay my crown at's feet, and there to kneel.
Tell him, from his all-obeying breath I hear
The doom of Egypt.
THIDIAS   'Tis your noblest course.
Wisdom and fortune combating together,
If that the former dare but what it can,   80
No chance may shake it. Give me grace to lay
My duty on your hand.   [*He begins to kiss her hand.*
CLEOPATRA   Your Cæsar's father oft
(When he hath mused of taking kingdoms in)
Bestowed his lips on that unworthy place,
As it rained kisses.

                    Enter ANTONY *and* ENOBARBUS.

ANTONY   [*seeing Thidias:*]   Favours, by Jove that thunders!
What art thou, fellow?
THIDIAS   One that but performs
The bidding of the fullest man and worthiest
To have command obeyed.
ENOBARB.   You will be whipped.
ANTONY   [*calling servants:*] Approach, there! [*To Cleopatra:*] Ah,
                    you kite! – Now, gods and devils!
Authority melts from me. Of late when I cried 'Ho!',   90
Like boys unto a muss, kings would start forth,
And cry 'Your will?'.

Enter SERVANTS.

	— Have you no ears? I am
	Antony yet. Take hence this Jack, and whip him.
ENOBARB.	[*to himself:*] 'Tis better playing with a lion's whelp
	Than with an old one dying.
ANTONY	Moon and stars!
	Whip him! Were't twenty of the greatest tributaries
	That do acknowledge Cæsar, should I find them
	So saucy with the hand of she here — what's her name
	Since she was Cleopatra? Whip him, fellows,
	Till like a boy you see him cringe his face, 100
	And whine aloud for mercy. Take him hence.
THIDIAS	Mark Antony —
ANTONY	Tug him away; being whipped,
	Bring him again. This Jack of Cæsar's shall
	Bear us an errand to him. [*Exeunt servants with Thidias.*
	[*To Cleopatra:*] You were half blasted ere I knew
	you. Ha!
	Have I my pillow left unpressed in Rome,
	Forborne the getting of a lawful race,
	And by a gem of women, to be abused
	By one that looks on feeders?
CLEOPATRA	Good my lord —
ANTONY	You have been a boggler ever, 110
	But when we in our viciousness grow hard
	(O misery on't!), the wise gods seel our eyes,
	In our own filth drop our clear judgements, make us
	Adore our errors, laugh at's while we strut
	To our confusion.
CLEOPATRA	O, is't come to this?
ANTONY	I found you as a morsel cold upon
	Dead Cæsar's trencher; nay, you were a fragment
	Of Gnæus Pompey's,[88] besides what hotter hours,
	Unregistered in vulgar fame, you have
	Luxuriously picked out: for I am sure, 120
	Though you can guess what temperance should be,
	You know not what it is.
CLEOPATRA	Wherefore is this?
ANTONY	To let a fellow that will take rewards

And say 'God quit you!' be familiar with
My playfellow, your hand, this kingly seal
And plighter of high hearts! O, that I were
Upon the hill of Basan, to outroar
The hornèd herd![89] For I have savage cause;
And to proclaim it civilly were like
A haltered neck which does the hangman thank   130
For being yare about him.

            Enter a SERVANT *with* THIDIAS.

                                   – Is he whipped?

SERVANT   Soundly, my lord.
ANTONY   Cried he? And begged a pardon?
SERVANT   He did ask favour.
ANTONY   [*To Thidias:*] If that thy father live, let him repent
Thou wast not made his daughter; and be thou sorry
To follow Cæsar in his triumph, since
Thou hast been whipped for following him.
                                     Henceforth
The white hand of a lady fever thee;
Shake thou to look on't. Get thee back to Cæsar;
Tell him thy entertainment: look thou say   140
He makes me angry with him. For he seems
Proud and disdainful, harping on what I am,
Not what he knew I was. He makes me angry;
And at this time most easy 'tis to do't,
When my good stars, that were my former guides,
Have empty left their orbs, and shot their fires
Into th'abysm of hell. If he mislike
My speech and what is done, tell him he has
Hipparchus, my enfranchèd bondman, whom
He may at pleasure whip, or hang, or torture,   150
As he shall like, to quit me. Urge it thou.
Hence with thy stripes, be gone!   [*Exit Thidias.*
CLEOPATRA Have you done yet?
ANTONY   Alack, our terrene moon
Is now eclipsed, and it portends alone
The fall of Antony.
CLEOPATRA   I must stay his time.

ANTONY   To flatter Cæsar, would you mingle eyes
            With one that ties his points?
CLEOPATRA   Not know me yet?
ANTONY   Cold-hearted toward me?
CLEOPATRA   Ah, dear, if I be so,
            From my cold heart let heaven engender hail,
            And poison it in the source, and the first stone   160
            Drop in my neck: as it determines, so
            Dissolve my life; the next, Cæsarion smite;
            Till by degrees the memory of my womb,
            Together with my brave Egyptians all,
            By the discandying of this pelleted storm
            Lie graveless, till the flies and gnats of Nile
            Have buried them for prey!
ANTONY   I am satisfied.
            Cæsar sets down in Alexandria, where
            I will oppose his fate. Our force by land
            Hath nobly held; severed navy too   170
            Have knit again, and fleet, threat'ning most sea-like.
            Where hast thou been, my heart? Dost thou hear, lady?
            If from the field I shall return once more
            To kiss these lips, I will appear in blood;
            I and my sword will earn our chronicle.
            There's hope in't yet.
CLEOPATRA That's my brave lord!
ANTONY   I will be treble-sinewed, hearted, breathed,
            And fight maliciously: for when mine hours
            Were nice and lucky, men did ransom lives   180
            Of me for jests; but now I'll set my teeth,
            And send to darkness all that stop me. Come,
            Let's have one other gaudy night. Call to me
            All my sad captains; fill our bowls once more:
            Let's mock the midnight bell.
CLEOPATRA   It is my birthday.
            I had thought t'have held it poor. But since my lord
            Is Antony again, I will be Cleopatra.
ANTONY   We will yet do well.
CLEOPATRA [to servant:] Call all his noble captains to my lord.
ANTONY   Do so.   [Exit servant.

We'll speak to them, and tonight I'll force   190
The wine peep through their scars. Come on,
                                                  my Queen;
There's sap in't yet. The next time I do fight
I'll make Death love me, for I will contend
Even with his pestilent scythe. [*Exeunt all but Enobarbus.*
ENOBARB. Now he'll outstare the lightning. To be furious
Is to be frighted out of fear, and in that mood
The dove will peck the estridge; and I see still
A diminution in our captain's brain
Restores his heart: when valour preys on reason,
It eats the sword it fights with. I will seek   200
Some way to leave him.   [*Exit.*

ACT 4, SCENE 1.

Near Alexandria. Cæsar's camp.

Enter CÆSAR *(reading a letter),* AGRIPPA *and* MÆCENAS,
with his ARMY.

CÆSAR He calls me boy, and chides as he had power
To beat me out of Egypt. My messenger
He hath whipped with rods; dares me to
personal combat,
Cæsar to Antony. Let the old ruffian know
I have many other ways to die; meantime
Laugh at his challenge.

MÆCENAS Cæsar must think,
When one so great begins to rage, he's hunted
Even to falling. Give him no breath, but now
Make boot of his distraction. Never anger
Made good guard for itself.

CÆSAR Let our best heads 10
Know that tomorrow the last of many battles
We mean to fight. Within our files there are,
Of those that served Mark Antony but late,
Enough to fetch him in. See it done,
And feast the army: we have store to do't,
And they have earned the waste. Poor Antony! [*Exeunt.*

SCENE 2.

Alexandria. Inside Cleopatra's palace.

Enter ANTONY, CLEOPATRA, ENOBARBUS, CHARMIAN,
IRAS, ALEXAS *and* OTHERS.

ANTONY He will not fight with me, Domitius?
ENOBARB. No.
ANTONY Why should he not?
ENOBARB. He thinks, being twenty times of better fortune,
He is twenty men to one.
ANTONY Tomorrow, soldier,

                    By sea and land I'll fight. Or I will live,
                    Or bathe my dying honour in the blood
                    Shall make it live again. Woot thou fight well?
ENOBARB.   I'll strike, and cry 'Take all!'.
ANTONY   Well said. Come on:
                    Call forth my household servants: let's tonight
                    Be bounteous at our meal.   [*Enobarbus calls.*

                         Enter six SERVANTS.

                    [*To servants in turn:*]   Give me thy hand: 10
                    Thou hast been rightly honest; so hast thou,
                    Thou, and thou, and thou. You have served me well,
                    And kings have been your fellows.
CLEOPATRA [*aside to Enobarbus:*]   What means this?
ENOBARB.   'Tis one of those odd tricks which sorrow shoots
                    Out of the mind.
ANTONY   [*to a servant:*]   And thou art honest too.
                    I wish I could be made so many men,
                    And all of you clapped up together in
                    An Antony, that I might do you service
                    So good as you have done.
SERVANTS   The gods forbid!
ANTONY   Well, my good fellows, wait on me tonight: 20
                    Scant not my cups, and make as much of me
                    As when mine empire was your fellow too
                    And suffered my command.
CLEOPATRA [*aside to Enobarbus:*]   What does he mean?
ENOBARB.   To make his followers weep.
ANTONY   [*to servants:*]   Tend me tonight;
                    May be it is the period of your duty.
                    Haply you shall not see me more; or if,
                    A mangled shadow. Perchance tomorrow
                    You'll serve another master. I look on you
                    As one that takes his leave. Mine honest friends,
                    I turn you not away; but, like a master   30
                    Married to your good service, stay till death.
                    Tend me tonight two hours, I ask no more,
                    And the gods yield you for't!
ENOBARB.   What mean you, sir,

  To give them this discomfort? Look, they weep,
  And I, an ass, am onion-eyed. For shame,
  Transform us not to women.
ANTONY   Ho, ho, ho!
  Now the witch take me, if I meant it thus!
  Grace grow where those drops fall! My hearty friends,
  You take me in too dolorous a sense;
  For I spake to you for your comfort, did desire you 40
  To burn this night with torches. Know, my hearts,
  I hope well of tomorrow, and will lead you
  Where rather I'll expect victorious life
  Than death and honour. Let's to supper, come,
  And drown consideration.   [*Exeunt.*

SCENE 3.

Alexandria. Near Cleopatra's palace.

Enter two SOLDIERS.[90]

SOLDIER 1 Brother, good night; tomorrow is the day.
SOLDIER 2 It will determine one way. Fare you well.
  Heard you of nothing strange about the streets?
SOLDIER 1 Nothing: what news?
SOLDIER 2 Belike 'tis but a rumour. Good night to you.
SOLDIER 1 Well sir, good night.

    Enter two SOLDIERS, *meeting them.*

SOLDIER 2 Soldiers, have careful watch.
SOLDIER 3 And you. Good night, good night.

    They place themselves in every corner.

SOLDIER 2 Here we; and if tomorrow
  Our navy thrive, I have an absolute hope 10
  Our landmen will stand up.
SOLDIER 1   'Tis a brave army,
  And full of purpose.

      [*Music of hautboys beneath.*[91]
SOLDIER 2   Peace! What noise?
SOLDIER 1   List, List!

SOLDIER 2 Hark!
SOLDIER 1   Music i'th'air.
SOLDIER 3   Under the earth.
SOLDIER 4 It signs well, does it not?
SOLDIER 3   No.
SOLDIER 1   Peace, I say!
What should this mean?
SOLDIER 2 'Tis the god Hercules, whom Antony loved,
Now leaves him.
SOLDIER 1   Walk: let's see if other watchmen
Do hear what we do.
SOLDIER 2   How now, masters!
ALL   [speaking together:]   How now?
How now? Do you hear this?
SOLDIER 1   Ay, is't not strange?
SOLDIER 3 Do you hear, masters? Do you hear?   20
SOLDIER 1 Follow the noise so far as we have quarter;
Let's see how it will give off.
ALL   Content. 'Tis strange.
                       [Exeunt.

SCENE 4.

Alexandria. Inside Cleopatra's palace.

Enter ANTONY, *followed by* CLEOPATRA *and* CHARMIAN.

ANTONY   [calling:] Eros! Mine armour, Eros!
CLEOPATRA   Sleep a little.
ANTONY   No, my chuck. – Eros, come; mine armour, Eros!

Enter EROS *with armour.*

Come, good fellow, put thine iron on.
If Fortune be not ours today, it is
Because we brave her. Come.
CLEOPATRA   Nay, I'll help too.
What's this for?   [She tries to equip him.
ANTONY   Ah, let be, let be! Thou art
The armourer of my heart. False, false; this, this.

CLEOPATRA Sooth, law, I'll help: thus it must be.[92]
ANTONY   Well, well,
          We shall thrive now. – Seest thou, my good fellow?
          Go put on thy defences.
EROS   Briefly, sir.   10
CLEOPATRA Is not this buckled well?
ANTONY   Rarely, rarely:
          He that unbuckles this, till we do please
          To daff't for our repose, shall hear a storm. –
          Thou fumblest, Eros; and my Queen's a squire
          More tight at this than thou: dispatch. – O love,
          That thou couldst see my wars today, and knew'st
          The royal occupation! Thou shouldst see
          A workman in't.

                    Enter an armed SOLDIER.

                         – Good morrow to thee: welcome.
          Thou look'st like him that knows a warlike charge:
          To business that we love we rise betime,   20
          And go to't with delight.
SOLDIER   A thousand, sir,
          Early though't be, have on their riveted trim,
          And at the port expect you. [*Shouts heard. Trumpets flourish.*

                    Enter CAPTAINS *and* SOLDIERS.

CAPTAIN   The morn is fair. Good morrow, General.
ALL   Good morrow, General.
ANTONY   'Tis well blown, lads.
          This morning, like the spirit of a youth
          That means to be of note, begins betimes.
          So, so. Come, give me that; this way; well said!
          – Fare thee well, dame; whate'er becomes of me,
          This is a soldier's kiss [*He kisses Cleopatra.*]: rebukable   30
          And worthy shameful check it were, to stand
          On more mechanic compliment. I'll leave thee
          Now like a man of steel. – You that will fight,
          Follow me close; I'll bring you to't. – Adieu.
                    [*Exeunt all except Cleopatra and Charmian.*
CHARMIAN Please you retire to your chamber?
CLEOPATRA   Lead me.

He goes forth gallantly. That he and Cæsar might
Determine this great war in single fight!
Then, Antony; but now. . . Well, on.   [*Exeunt.*

SCENE 5.

Near Alexandria. Antony's camp.

Trumpets sound. Enter ANTONY, EROS, *and a* SOLDIER *meeting them.*[93]

SOLDIER	The gods make this a happy day to Antony!
ANTONY	Would thou and those thy scars had once prevailed
	To make me fight at land!
SOLDIER	Hadst thou done so,

SOLDIER   Hadst thou done so,
The kings that have revolted, and the soldier
That has this morning left thee, would have still
Followed thy heels.

ANTONY   Who's gone this morning?

SOLDIER   Who?
One ever near thee. Call for Enobarbus,
He shall not hear thee; or from Cæsar's camp
Say 'I am none of thine'.

ANTONY   What sayest thou?

SOLDIER   Sir,
He is with Cæsar.

EROS   Sir, his chests and treasure   10
He has not with him.

ANTONY   Is he gone?

SOLDIER   Most certain.

ANTONY   Go, Eros, send his treasure after; do it;
Detain no jot, I charge thee. Write to him
(I will subscribe) gentle adieus and greetings;
Say that I wish he never find more cause
To change a master. – O, my fortunes have
Corrupted honest men! – Dispatch. – Enobarbus!
                                   [*Exeunt.*

SCENE 6.

Near Alexandria. Cæsar's camp.

Flourish. Enter CÆSAR, AGRIPPA, ENOBARBUS *and* DOLABELLA.

CÆSAR Go forth, Agrippa, and begin the fight.
Our will is Antony be took alive;
Make it so known.

AGRIPPA Cæsar, I shall.   [*Exit.*

CÆSAR The time of universal peace is near:
Prove this a prosp'rous day, the three-nooked world
Shall bear the olive freely.[94]

Enter a MESSENGER.

MESSEN.   Antony
Is come into the field.

CÆSAR   Go charge Agrippa
Plant those that have revolted in the vant,
That Antony may seem to spend his fury   10
Upon himself.   [*Exeunt all except Enobarbus.*

ENOBARB. Alexas did revolt, and went to Jewry on
Affairs of Antony; there did dissuade
Great Herod to incline himself to Cæsar
And leave his master Antony. For this pains
Cæsar hath hanged him.[95] Canidius and the rest
That fell away have entertainment, but
No honourable trust. I have done ill,
Of which I do accuse myself so sorely
That I will joy no more.

Enter a SOLDIER *of Cæsar's.*

SOLDIER   Enobarbus, Antony   20
Hath after thee sent all thy treasure, with
His bounty over-plus. The messenger
Came on my guard, and at thy tent is now
Unloading of his mules.

ENOBARB.   I give it you.

SOLDIER Mock not, Enobarbus:

I tell you true. Best you safed the bringer
Out of the host. I must attend mine office,
Or would have done't myself. Your Emperor
Continues still a Jove.   [*Exit.*

ENOBARB.   I am alone the villain of the earth,   30
And feel I am so most. O Antony,
Thou mine of bounty, how wouldst thou have paid
My better service, when my turpitude
Thou dost so crown with gold! This blows my heart.
If swift thought break it not, a swifter mean
Shall outstrike thought; but thought will do't, I feel.
I fight against thee? No, I will go seek
Some ditch wherein to die: the foul'st best fits
My latter part of life.   [*Exit.*

SCENE 7.

Near Alexandria. The battlefield.

Alarum. Drums and trumpets are heard. Enter AGRIPPA *and* OTHERS.

AGRIPPA   Retire! We have engaged ourselves too far:
Cæsar himself has work, and our oppression
Exceeds what we expected.   [*Exeunt.*

Alarums. Enter SCARRUS *(wounded) with* ANTONY.

SCARRUS   O my brave Emperor, this is fought indeed!
Had we done so at first, we had droven them home
With clouts about their heads.

ANTONY   Thou bleed'st apace.

SCARRUS   I had a wound here that was like a 'T',
But now 'tis made an 'H'.[96]   [*Retreat sounded far off.*

ANTONY   They do retire.

SCARRUS   We'll beat 'em into bench-holes. I have yet
Room for six scotches more.   10

Enter EROS.

EROS   They are beaten, sir, and our advantage serves
For a fair victory.

SCARRUS   Let us score their backs

And snatch 'em up, as we take hares, behind:
'Tis sport to maul a runner.

ANTONY   I will reward thee
Once for thy sprightly comfort, and ten-fold
For thy good valour. Come thee on.

SCARRUS   I'll halt after.

                                        [*Exeunt.*

SCENE 8.

Near the battlefield.

Alarum. Enter ANTONY, SCARRUS *and* SOLDIERS, *marching
as from victory, with drums and trumpets. They halt.*

ANTONY   We have beat him to his camp. Run one before,
And let the Queen know of our gests.   [*Exit soldier.*
                                        Tomorrow,
Before the sun shall see's, we'll spill the blood
That has today escaped. I thank you all,
For doughty-handed are you, and have fought
Not as you served the cause, but as't had been
Each man's like mine; you have shown all Hectors.[97]
Enter the city, clip your wives, your friends;
Tell them your feats; whilst they with joyful tears
Wash the congealment from your wounds, and kiss   10
The honoured gashes whole.

                    Enter CLEOPATRA.

                    [*To Scarrus:*] Give me thy hand:
To this great fairy I'll commend thy acts,
Make her thanks bless thee. [*To Cleopatra:*] O thou
                                        day o'th'world,
Chain mine armed neck; leap thou, attire and all,
Through proof of harness to my heart, and there
Ride on the pants triúmphing!

CLEOPATRA   Lord of lords!
O infinite virtue, com'st thou smiling from
The world's great snare uncaught?

ANTONY   My nightingale,

We have beat them to their beds. What, girl:
                                  Though grey
Do something mingle with our younger brown,   20
                                  yet ha'we
A brain that nourishes our nerves and can
Get goal for goal of youth. Behold this man;
Commend unto his lips thy favouring hand:
Kiss it, my warrior: he hath fought today
As if a god, in hate of mankind, had
Destroyed in such a shape.   [*Scarrus kisses her hand.*

CLEOPATRA [*to Scarrus:*]   I'll give thee, friend,
An armour all of gold; it was a king's.

ANTONY He has deserved it, were it cárbuncled
Like holy Phoebus' car. Give me thy hand.   30
Through Alexandria make a jolly march;
Bear our hacked targets like the men that owe them.
Had our great palace the capacity
To camp this host, we all would sup together
And drink carouses to the next day's fate,
Which promises royal peril. [*He calls:*] Trumpeters,
With brazen din blast you the city's ear,
Make mingle with our rattling tabourines,
That heaven and earth may strike their sounds together,
Applauding our approach!
                      [*Loud fanfare sounds. Exeunt.*

SCENE 9.

Near Alexandria. Cæsar's camp.

Enter a SENTRY *and his company of* WATCHMEN.
Enter, separately, ENOBARBUS.

SENTRY If we be not relieved within this hour,
We must return to th'court of guard: the night
Is shiny, and they say we shall embattle
By th'second hour i'th'morn.

WATCH. I   This last day was
A shrewd one to's.

ENOBARB.   O, bear me witness, night.

WATCH. 2 What man is this?
WATCH. 1   Stand close, and list him.
                                              [*They eavesdrop.*
ENOBARB. Be witness to me, O thou blessed moon.
          When men revolted shall upon recórd
          Bear hateful memory, poor Enobarbus did   10
          Before thy face repent.
SENTRY   Enobarbus?
WATCH. 2 Peace: hark further.
ENOBARB. O sovereign mistress of true melancholy,
          The poisonous damp of night disponge upon me,
          That life, a very rebel to my will,
          May hang no longer on me. Throw my heart
          Against the flint and hardness of my fault,
          Which, being dried with grief, will break to powder,
          And finish all foul thoughts. – O Antony,   20
          Nobler than my revolt is infamous,
          Forgive me in thine own particular,
          But let the world rank me in register
          A master-leaver and a fugitive.
          O Antony! O Antony!   [*He dies.*
WATCH. 1   Let's speak to him.
SENTRY   Let's hear him, for the things he speaks
          May concern Cæsar.
WATCH. 2   Let's do so. But he sleeps.
SENTRY   Swoonds rather; for so bad a prayer as his
          Was never yet for sleep.
WATCH. 1   Go we to him.
WATCH. 2 Awake, sir, awake. Speak to us.
WATCH. 1   Hear you, sir?
SENTRY   The hand of death hath raught him.   [*Drums far off.* 30
                                       Hark: the drums
          Demurely wake the sleepers. Let's bear him
          To th'court of guard: he is of note. Our hour
          Is fully out.
WATCH. 2 Come on, then; he may recover yet.
                              [*Exeunt, bearing Enobarbus.*

SCENE 10.

Near Alexandria.

Enter ANTONY *and* SCARRUS, *with their* ARMY.

ANTONY   Their preparation is today by sea:
We please them not by land.

SCARRUS   For both, my lord.

ANTONY   I would they'd fight i'th'fire or i'th'air;[98]
We'd fight there too. But this it is, our foot
Upon the hills adjoining to the city
Shall stay with us (order for sea is given;
They have put forth the haven),
Where their appointment we may best discover,
And look on their endeavour.   [*Exeunt.*

SCENE 11.

Near Alexandria.

Enter CÆSAR *and his* ARMY.

CÆSAR   But being charged, we will be still by land;
Which, as I take't, we shall, for his best force
Is forth to man his galleys. To the vales,
And hold our best advantage.   [*Exeunt.*

SCENE 12.

A hill near Alexandria.

Enter ANTONY *and* SCARRUS.

ANTONY   Yet they are not joined. Where yond pine does stand,
I shall discover all: I'll bring thee word
Straight, how 'tis like to go.   [*Exit.*

SCARRUS   Swallows have built
In Cleopatra's sails their nests.[99] The augurers

Say they know not, they cannot tell; look grimly,
And dare not speak their knowledge. Antony
Is valiant and dejected, and by starts
His fretted fortunes give him hope and fear,
Of what he has and has not.

Alarum far off. The sea-battle proceeds and ends.[100]

Enter ANTONY.

ANTONY   All is lost!
This foul Egyptian hath betrayèd me: 10
My fleet hath yielded to the foe, and yonder
They cast their caps up and carouse together
Like friends long lost. – Triple-turned whore, 'tis thou
Hast sold me to this novice; and my heart
Makes only wars on thee! [*To Scarrus:*] Bid them all fly;
For when I am revenged upon my charm,
I have done all. Bid them all fly: be gone! [*Exit Scarrus.*
O sun, thy uprise shall I see no more.
Fortune and Antony part here; even here
Do we shake hands. All come to this? The hearts   20
That spanieled me at heels, to whom I gave
Their wishes, do discandy, melt their sweets
On blossoming Cæsar; and this pine is barked,
That overtopped them all. Betrayed I am.[101]
O this false soul of Egypt! This grave charm,
Whose eye becked forth my wars and called
                                                                  them home,
Whose bosom was my crownet, my chief end,
Like a right gypsy hath at fast and loose
Beguiled me to the very heart of loss.
[*He calls:*] What, Eros, Eros!

Enter CLEOPATRA.

                                          Ah, thou spell! Avaunt!   30
CLEOPATRA Why is my lord enraged against his love?
ANTONY   Vanish, or I shall give thee thy deserving,
          And blemish Cæsar's triumph. Let him take thee,
          And hoist thee up to the shouting plébeians;
          Follow his chariot, like the greatest spot
          Of all thy sex. Most monster-like, be shown

For poor'st diminutives, for dolts,[102] and let
Patient Octavia plough thy visage up
With her preparèd nails.   [*Exit Cleopatra.*
                              'Tis well thou'rt gone,
If it be well to live; but better 'twere   40
Thou fell'st into my fury, for one death
Might have prevented many. – Eros, ho! –
The shirt of Nessus is upon me: teach me,
Alcides, thou mine ancestor, thy rage.
Let me lodge Lichas on the horns o'th'moon,
And, with those hands that grasped the heaviest club,
Subdue my worthiest self.[103] – The witch shall die.
To the young Roman boy she hath sold me, and I fall
Under this plot. She dies for't. – Eros, ho!   [*Exit.*

SCENE 13.

Alexandria. Cleopatra's palace.

Enter CLEOPATRA, CHARMIAN, IRAS *and* MARDIAN.

CLEOPATRA Help me, my women! O, he's more mad
          Than Telamon for his shield; the Boar of Thessaly
          Was never so embossed.[104]
CHARMIAN   To th'monument.
          There lock yourself, and send him word you are dead.
          The soul and body rive not more in parting
          Than greatness going off.
CLEOPATRA   To th'monument!
          – Mardian, go tell him I have slain myself;
          Say that the last I spoke was 'Antony',
          And word it (prithee) piteously. Hence, Mardian,
          And bring me how he takes my death.
                              To th'monument! [*Exeunt* 10

SCENE 14.

Alexandria. Cleopatra's palace.

Enter ANTONY *and* EROS.

ANTONY   Eros, thou yet behold'st me?

EROS   Ay, noble lord.

ANTONY   Sometime we see a cloud that's dragonish,
A vapour sometime like a bear or lion,
A towered citadel, a pendent rock,
A forkèd mountain, or blue promontory
With trees upon't, that nod unto the world,
And mock our eyes with air. Thou hast seen these signs;
They are black Vesper's pageants.

EROS   Ay, my lord.

ANTONY   That which is now a horse, even with a thought
The rack dislimns, and makes it indistinct   10
As water is in water.

EROS   It does, my lord.

ANTONY   My good knave Eros, now thy captain is
Even such a body: here I am Antony,
Yet cannot hold this visible shape, my knave.
I made these wars for Egypt, and the Queen –
Whose heart I thought I had, for she had mine,
Which, whilst it was mine, had annexed unto't
A million moe (now lost) – she, Eros, has
Packed cards with Cæsar, and false-played my glory
Unto an enemy's triumph.[105]   20
Nay, weep not, gentle Eros, there is left us
Ourselves to end ourselves.

Enter MARDIAN.

                      – O, thy vilde lady!
She has robbed me of my sword.

MARDIAN   No, Antony,
My mistress loved thee, and her fortunes mingled
With thine entirely.

ANTONY   Hence, saucy eunuch! Peace!

She hath betrayed me, and shall die the death.
MARDIAN Death of one person can be paid but once,
And that she has discharged. What thou wouldst do
Is done unto thy hand: the last she spake
Was 'Antony! Most noble Antony!';   30
Then in the midst a tearing groan did break
The name of Antony: it was divided
Between her heart and lips: she rendered life,
Thy name so buried in her.
ANTONY   Dead then?
MARDIAN   Dead.
ANTONY – Unarm, Eros, the long day's task is done,
And we must sleep. [*To Mardian:*] That thou depart'st
                                                                hence safe
Does pay thy labour richly. Go.   [*Exit Mardian.*
Off, pluck off.   [*Eros helps Antony to disarm.*
The seven-fold shield of Ajax cannot keep
This battery from my heart.[106] O, cleave, my sides!   40
Heart, once be stronger than thy continent:
Crack thy frail case! Apace, Eros, apace! [*He is disarmed.*
No more a soldier. Bruisèd pieces, go;
You have been nobly borne. [*To Eros:*] From me awhile.
                                                        [*Exit Eros.*

I will o'ertake thee, Cleopatra, and
Weep for my pardon. So it must be, for now
All length is torture: since the torch is out,
Lie down and stray no farther. Now all labour
Mars what it does; yea, very force entangles
Itself with strength. Seal then, and all is done.   50
– Eros! – I come, my Queen. – Eros! – Stay for me.
Where souls do couch on flowers, we'll hand in hand,
And with our sprightly port make the ghosts gaze:
Dido and her Æneas shall want troops,
And all the haunt be ours.[107] – Come, Eros, Eros!

                          Enter EROS.

EROS   What would my lord?
ANTONY   Since Cleopatra died,
I have lived in such dishonour that the gods

Detest my baseness. I, that with my sword
Quartered the world, and o'er green Neptune's back
With ships made cities, condemn myself to lack   60
The courage of a woman: less noble mind
Than she which, by her death, our Cæsar tells
'I am conqueror of myself'. Thou art sworn, Eros,
That when the exigent should come (which now
Is come indeed), when I should see behind me
Th'inevitable prosecution of
Disgrace and horror, that, on my command,
Thou then wouldst kill me. Do't: the time is come;
Thou strik'st not me, 'tis Cæsar thou defeat'st.
Put colour in thy cheek.

EROS   The gods withhold me!   70
Shall I do that which all the Parthian darts,
Though enemy, lost aim and could not?

ANTONY   Eros,
Wouldst thou be windowed in great Rome, and see
Thy master thus with pleached arms, bending down
His corrigible neck, his face subdued
To penetrative shame, whilst the wheeled seat
Of fortunate Cæsar, drawn before him, branded
His baseness that ensued? [108]

EROS   I would not see't.

ANTONY Come then; for with a wound I must be cured.
Draw that thy honest sword, which thou hast worn   80
Most useful for thy country.

EROS   O sir, pardon me!

ANTONY When I did make thee free, swor'st thou not then
To do this when I bade thee? Do it at once,
Or thy precédent services are all
But accidents unpurposed. Draw, and come.

EROS Turn from me then that noble countenance,
Wherein the worship of the whole world lies.

ANTONY [turning:] Lo thee.

EROS My sword is drawn.

ANTONY   Then let it do at once
The thing why thou hast drawn it.

EROS   My dear master,   90

	My captain, and my Emperor, let me say,
	Before I strike this bloody stroke 'Farewell'.
ANTONY	'Tis said, man; and farewell.
EROS	Farewell, great chief. Shall I strike now?
ANTONY	Now, Eros.

                                                            [Eros stabs himself.

EROS   Why, there then. Thus I do escape the sorrow
              Of Antony's death.   *[He dies.*

ANTONY   Thrice-nobler than myself!
              Thou teachest me, O valiant Eros, what
              I should and thou couldst not. My Queen and Eros
              Have by their brave instruction got upon me
              A nobleness in recórd; but I will be   100
              A bridegroom in my death, and run into't
              As to a lover's bed. Come then; and, Eros,
              Thy master dies thy scholar: to do thus

                                                       [He stabs himself.

              I learnt of thee. — How, not dead? Not dead?
              — The guard, ho! O, dispatch me!

                     Enter DERCETUS[109] *and* GUARDS.

GUARD I		What's the noise?
ANTONY	I have done my work ill, friends: O, make an end	
	Of what I have begun.	
GUARD 2	The star is fall'n.	
GUARD I	And time is at his period.	
GUARDS	Alas, and woe!	
ANTONY	Let him that loves me strike me dead.	
GUARD I	Not I.	
GUARD 2	Nor I.	
GUARD 3	Nor any one. *[Exeunt guards.*	110
DERCETUS	Thy death and fortunes bid thy followers fly.	
	This sword but shown to Cæsar, with this tidings,	
	Shall enter me with him. *[He takes Antony's sword.*	

                           Enter DIOMEDES.

DIOMEDES	Where's Antony?
DERCETUS	There, Diomed, there.
DIOMEDES	Lives he?
	Wilt thou not answer, man? *[Exit Dercetus.*

ANTONY   Art thou there, Diomed? Draw thy sword, and give me
            Sufficing strokes for death.
DIOMEDES   Most absolute lord,
            My mistress Cleopatra sent me to thee.
ANTONY   When did she send thee?
DIOMEDES   Now, my lord.
ANTONY   Where is she?
DIOMEDES   Locked in her monument. She had a prophesying fear   120
            Of what hath come to pass: for when she saw
            (Which never shall be found) you did suspect
            She had disposed with Cæsar, and that your rage
            Would not be purged, she sent you word she was dead;
            But fearing since how it might work, hath sent
            Me to proclaim the truth; and I am come,
            I dread, too late.
ANTONY   Too late, good Diomed: call my guard, I prithee.
DIOMEDES   What ho, the Emperor's guard! The guard, what ho!
            Come, your lord calls.   130

            Enter four or five of Antony's GUARDS.

ANTONY   Bear me, good friends, where Cleopatra bides.
            'Tis the last service that I shall command you.
GUARD 1   Woe, woe are we, sir. You may not live to wear
            All your true followers out.
GUARDS   Most heavy day!
ANTONY   Nay, good my fellows, do not please sharp fate
            To grace it with your sorrows. Bid that welcome
            Which comes to punish us, and we punish it,
            Seeming to bear it lightly. Take me up.
            I have led you oft; carry me now, good friends,
            And have my thanks for all.   140
                        [*Exeunt, Antony and Eros carried by guards.*

SCENE 15.

Alexandria. Cleopatra's monument.

Enter, above, CLEOPATRA, CHARMIAN, IRAS *and* MAIDS.

CLEOPATRA O Charmian, I will never go from hence.

CHARMIAN Be comforted, dear madam.

CLEOPATRA   No, I will not:
All strange and terrible events are welcome,
But comforts we despise; our size of sorrow,
Proportioned to our cause, must be as great
As that which makes it.

                    Enter, below, DIOMEDES.

                              – How now? Is he dead?

DIOMEDES His death's upon him, but not dead.
Look out o'th'other side your monument:
His guard have brought him thither.

              Enter, below, ANTONY, *carried by* GUARDS.

CLEOPATRA   O sun,
Burn the great sphere thou mov'st in; darkling stand   10
The varying shore o'th'world! O Antony,
Antony, Antony! Help, Charmian; help, Iras, help;
Help, friends below, let's draw him hither.

ANTONY   Peace;
Not Cæsar's valour hath o'erthrown Antony,
But Antony's hath triumphed on itself.

CLEOPATRA So it should be, that none but Antony
Should conquer Antony; but woe 'tis so!

ANTONY I am dying, Egypt, dying; only
I here impórtune death awhile, until,
Of many thousand kisses, the poor last   20
I lay upon thy lips.

CLEOPATRA   I dare not, dear.
Dear my lord, pardon: I dare not,
Lest I be taken. Not th'imperious show
Of the full-fortuned Cæsar ever shall
Be brooched with me, if knife, drugs, serpents, have

Edge, sting, or operation. I am safe:
Your wife Octavia, with her modest eyes
And still conclusion, shall acquire no honour
Demuring upon me. But come, come, Antony –
Help me, my women – we must draw thee up.   30
– Assist, good friends. [*With ropes, they start to raise him.*

ANTONY   O, quick, or I am gone.

CLEOPATRA Here's sport indeed: how heavy weighs my lord!
Our strength is all gone into heaviness,
That makes the weight. Had I great Juno's power,
The strong-winged Mercury should fetch thee up
And set thee by Jove's side. Yet come a little;
Wishers were ever fools. O come, come, come.
                              [*Antony arrives above.*
And welcome, welcome! Die where thou hast lived.
Quicken with kissing: had my lips that power,
Thus would I wear them out.   [*She kisses him.*

OTHERS   A heavy sight.   40

ANTONY   I am dying, Egypt, dying.
Give me some wine, and let me speak a little.

CLEOPATRA No, let me speak, and let me rail so high
That the false huswife Fortune break her wheel,
Provoked by my offence.[110]

ANTONY   One word, sweet Queen:
Of Cæsar seek your honour, with your safety. O . . .

CLEOPATRA They do not go together.

ANTONY   Gentle, hear me:
None about Cæsar trust but Proculeius.

CLEOPATRA My resolution and my hands I'll trust;
None about Cæsar.   50

ANTONY   The miserable change now, at my end,
Lament nor sorrow at; but please your thoughts
In feeding them with those my former fortunes
Wherein I lived. The greatest prince o'th'world,
The noblest; and do now not basely die,
Not cowardly put off my helmet to
My countryman. A Roman, by a Roman
Valiantly vanquished. Now my spirit is going;
I can no more.

CLEOPATRA   Noblest of men, woot die?
Hast thou no care of me? Shall I abide   60
In this dull world, which in thy absence is
No better than a sty? – O see, my women:[*Antony dies.*
The crown o'th'earth doth melt. – My lord? –
O, withered is the garland of the war;
The soldier's pole is fall'n: young boys and girls
Are level now with men: the odds is gone,
And there is nothing left remarkable
Beneath the visiting moon.

CHARMIAN   O quietness, lady! [*Cleopatra faints.*

IRAS   She's dead too, our sovereign.

CHARMIAN   Lady!

IRAS   Madam!

CHARMIAN O madam, madam, madam.   70

IRAS   Royal Egypt, Empress!   [*Cleopatra recovers.*

CHARMIAN Peace, peace, Iras.

CLEOPATRA No more but e'en a woman, and commanded
By such poor passion as the maid that milks
And does the meanest chares. It were for me
To throw my sceptre at the injurious gods,
To tell them that this world did equal theirs
Till they had stol'n our jewel. All's but naught;
Patience is sottish, and impatience does
Become a dog that's mad: then is it sin   80
To rush into the secret house of Death,
Ere Death dare come to us? How do you, women?
What, what good cheer? Why, how now, Charmian?
My noble girls! Ah, women, women! Look,
Our lamp is spent; it's out. Good sirs, take heart:
We'll bury him; and then, what's brave, what's noble,
Let's do it after the high Roman fashion,
And make Death proud to take us. Come, away.
This case of that huge spirit now is cold.
Ah, women, women! Come; we have no friend   90
But resolution and the briefest end.
                    [*Exeunt, some above carrying Antony's body.*

ACT 5, SCENE 1.

Alexandria. Cæsar's camp.

Enter CÆSAR *with his Council of War:* AGRIPPA, DOLABELLA,
MÆCENAS, GALLUS *and* PROCULEIUS.

CÆSAR   Go to him, Dolabella: bid him yield.
           Being so frustrate, tell him, he mocks
           The pauses that he makes.[111]

DOLABELL.   Cæsar, I shall.   [*Exit.*

Enter DERCETUS *with the sword of Antony.*

CÆSAR   Wherefore is that? And what art thou that dar'st
           Appear thus to us?

DERCETUS   I am called Dercetus.
           Mark Antony I served, who best was worthy
           Best to be served: whilst he stood up and spoke,
           He was my master, and I wore my life
           To spend upon his haters. If thou please
           To take me to thee, as I was to him   10
           I'll be to Cæsar; if thou pleasest not,
           I yield thee up my life.

CÆSAR   What is't thou say'st?

DERCETUS   I say, O Cæsar, Antony is dead.

CÆSAR   The breaking of so great a thing should make
           A greater crack. The round world
           Should have shook lions into civil streets,
           And citizens to their dens. The death of Antony
           Is not a single doom; in that name lay
           A moiety of the world.

DERCETUS   He is dead, Cæsar,
           Not by a public minister of justice,   20
           Nor by a hired knife; but that self hand
           Which writ his honour in the acts it did
           Hath, with the courage which the heart did lend it,
           Splitted the heart. This is his sword;
           I robbed his wound of it: behold it stained
           With his most noble blood.

CÆSAR   Look you sad, friends?

The gods rebuke me, but it is tidings
To wash the eyes of kings.

AGRIPPA   And strange it is
That nature must compel us to lament
Our most persisted deeds.

MÆCENAS   His taints and honours   30
Waged equal with him.

AGRIPPA   A rarer spirit never
Did steer humanity; but you gods will give us
Some faults to make us men. Cæsar is touched.

MÆCENAS When such a spacious mirror's set before him,
He needs must see himself.

CÆSAR   O Antony,
I have followed thee to this; but we do launch
Diseases in our bodies. I must perforce
Have shown to thee such a declining day,
Or look on thine: we could not stall together
In the whole world. But yet let me lament,   40
With tears as sovereign as the blood of hearts,
That thou, my brother, my competitor
In top of all design, my mate in empire,
Friend and companion in the front of war,
The arm of mine own body, and the heart
Where mine his thoughts did kindle: that our stars,
Unreconciliable, should divide
Our equalness to this.[112] Hear me, good friends —

Enter an EGYPTIAN.

But I will tell you at some meeter season.
The business of this man looks out of him;   50
We'll hear him what he says. — Whence are you?

EGYPTIAN A poor Egyptian, yet the Queen my mistress,
Confined in all she has, her monument,
Of thy intents desires instruction,
That she preparèdly may frame herself
To th'way she's forced to.

CÆSAR   Bid her have good heart:
She soon shall know of us, by some of ours,
How honourable and how kindly we
Determine for her; for Cæsar cannot lean

To be ungentle.[113]

EGYPTIAN   So the gods preserve thee!   [*Exit.* 60

CÆSAR   Come hither, Proculeius. Go and say,
We purpose her no shame; give her what comforts
The quality of her passion shall require,
Lest, in her greatness, by some mortal stroke
She do defeat us; for her life in Rome
Would be eternal in our triumph. Go,
And with your speediest bring us what she says
And how you find of her.

PROCUL.   Cæsar, I shall.   [*Exit.*

CÆSAR   Gallus, go you along.   [*Exit Gallus.*
                    – Where's Dolabella,
To second Proculeius?

AGRIPPA, MÆCENAS   Dolabella!   70

CÆSAR   Let him alone; for I remember now
How he's employed. He shall in time be ready.
Go with me to my tent, where you shall see
How hardly I was drawn into this war,
How calm and gentle I proceeded still,
In all my writings. Go with me, and see
What I can show in this.   [*Exeunt.*

SCENE 2.

Alexandria. Cleopatra's monument.

Enter, inside the monument's entrance, CLEOPATRA, CHARMIAN,
IRAS *and* MARDIAN.

CLEOPATRA My desolation does begin to make
A better life. 'Tis paltry to be Cæsar:
Not being Fortune, he's but Fortune's knave,
A minister of her will; and it is great
To do that thing that ends all other deeds,
Which shackles accidents and bolts up change;
Which sleeps, and never palates more the dung,
The beggar's nurse and Cæsar's.[114]

Enter PROCULEIUS. *He approaches, from outside, the*
monument's entrance.

PROCUL.   Cæsar sends greeting to the Queen of Egypt,
And bids thee study on what fair demands   10
Thou mean'st to have him grant thee.

CLEOPATRA   What's thy name?

PROCUL.   My name is Proculeius.

CLEOPATRA   Antony
Did tell me of you, bade me trust you; but
I do not greatly care to be deceived,
That have no use for trusting. If your master
Would have a queen his beggar, you must tell him
That majesty, to keep decorum, must
No less beg than a kingdom: if he please
To give me conquered Egypt for my son,
He gives me so much of mine own as I   20
Will kneel to him with thanks.

PROCUL.   Be of good cheer:
Y'are fall'n into a princely hand; fear nothing;
Make your full reference freely to my lord,
Who is so full of grace that it flows over
On all that need. Let me report to him
Your sweet dependency, and you shall find
A conqueror that will pray in aid for kindness,[115]
Where he for grace is kneeled to.

CLEOPATRA   Pray you, tell him
I am his fortune's vassal, and I send him
The greatness he has got. I hourly learn   30
A doctrine of obedience, and would gladly
Look him i'th'face.

PROCUL.   This I'll report, dear lady.
Have comfort, for I know your plight is pitied
Of him that caused it.

Inside the monument, SOLDIERS, *led by* GALLUS, *rapidly approach.*[116]

GALLUS   [*to soldiers:*] You see how easily she may be surprised.
Guard her till Cæsar come.   [*Exit Gallus.*

IRAS   Royal Queen!

CHARMIAN O Cleopatra, thou art taken, Queen!

CLEOPATRA Quick, quick, good hands.   [*She draws a dagger.*

PROCUL.   Hold, worthy lady, hold:
                              [*He disarms her.*
Do not your self such wrong, who are in this   40
Relieved, but not betrayed.

CLEOPATRA   What, of death too,
That rids our dogs of languish?

PROCUL.   Cleopatra,
Do not abuse my master's bounty by
Th'undoing of your self: let the world see
His nobleness well acted, which your death
Will never let come forth.

CLEOPATRA   Where art thou, Death?
Come hither, come! Come, come, and take a queen
Worth many babes and beggars!

PROCUL.   O temperance, lady!

CLEOPATRA Sir, I will eat no meat, I'll not drink, sir;
If idle talk will once be necessary,   50
I'll not sleep neither.[117] This mortal house I'll ruin,
Do Cæsar what he can. Know, sir, that I
Will not wait pinioned at your master's court,
Nor once be chástised with the sober eye
Of dull Octavia. Shall they hoist me up
And show me to the shouting varletry
Of censuring Rome? Rather a ditch in Egypt
Be gentle grave unto me; rather on Nilus' mud
Lay me stark-nak'd, and let the water-flies
Blow me into abhorring; rather make   60
My country's high pyrámides my gibbet,
And hang me up in chains![118]

PROCUL.   You do extend
These thoughts of horror further than you shall
Find cause in Cæsar.

Enter DOLABELLA.

DOLABELL.   Proculeius,
What thou hast done, thy master Cæsar knows,
And he hath sent for thee. For the Queen,
I'll take her to my guard.

PROCUL.   So, Dolabella,
It shall content me best. Be gentle to her.
[*To Cleopatra:*] To Cæsar I will speak what you shall
                                please,
If you'll employ me to him.

CLEOPATRA   Say, I would die.   70
                              [*Exit Proculeius.*

DOLABELL. Most noble Empress, you have heard of me?
CLEOPATRA I cannot tell.
DOLABELL.   Assuredly you know me.
CLEOPATRA No matter, sir, what I have heard or known.
You laugh when boys or women tell their dreams;
Is't not your trick?
DOLABELL.   I understand not, madam.
CLEOPATRA I dreamt there was an Emperor Antony.
O, such another sleep, that I might see
But such another man!
DOLABELL.   If it might please ye –
CLEOPATRA His face was as the heav'ns, and therein stuck
A sun and moon, which kept their course and lighted   80
The little O, the earth.[119]
DOLABELL.   Most sovereign creature –
CLEOPATRA His legs bestrid the ocean, his reared arm
Crested the world; his voice was propertied
As all the tunèd spheres,[120] and that to friends;
But when he meant to quail and shake the orb,
He was as rattling thunder. For his bounty,
There was no winter in't: an autumn 'twas
That grew the more by reaping. His delights
Were dolphin-like: they showed his back above
The element they lived in. In his livery   90
Walked crowns and crownets; realms and islands were
As plates dropped from his pocket.[121]
DOLABELL.   Cleopatra –
CLEOPATRA Think you there was, or might be, such a man
As this I dreamt of?
DOLABELL.   Gentle madam, no.
CLEOPATRA You lie, up to the hearing of the gods!
But if there be, or ever were, one such,

It's past the size of dreaming. Nature wants stuff
To vie strange forms with Fancy; yet t'imagine
An Antony were Nature's piece 'gainst Fancy,
Condemning shadows quite.[122]

DOLABELL.   Hear me, good madam.   100
Your loss is as yourself, great; and you bear it
As answering to the weight. Would I might never
O'ertake pursued success, but I do feel,
By the rebound of yours, a grief that smites
My very heart at root.

CLEOPATRA   I thank you, sir.
Know you what Cæsar means to do with me?

DOLABELL. I am loath to tell you what I would you knew.

CLEOPATRA Nay, pray you, sir.

DOLABELL.   Though he be honourable –

CLEOPATRA He'll lead me then in triumph?

DOLABELL. Madam, he will, I know't.   [Flourish.

SHOUTING HEARD   Make way there! Cæsar!   110

Enter CÆSAR *with* GALLUS, PROCULEIUS, MÆCENAS,
and other FOLLOWERS.

CÆSAR   Which is the Queen of Egypt?

DOLABELL. It is the Emperor, madam.   [Cleopatra kneels.

CÆSAR   Arise, you shall not kneel:
I pray you, rise; rise, Egypt.

CLEOPATRA [rising:]   Sir, the gods
Will have it thus: my master and my lord
I must obey.

CÆSAR   Take to you no hard thoughts.
The record of what injuries you did us,
Though written in our flesh, we shall remember
As things but done by chance.

CLEOPATRA   Sole Sir o'th'world,
I cannot próject mine own cause so well   120
To make it clear, but do confess I have
Been laden with like frailties which before
Have often shamed our sex.

CÆSAR   Cleopatra, know,
We will extenuate rather than enforce:
If you apply yourself to our intents,

Which towards you are most gentle, you shall find
A benefit in this change; but if you seek
To lay on me a cruelty by taking
Antony's course, you shall bereave yourself
Of my good purposes and put your children   130
To that destruction which I'll guard them from,
If thereon you rely. I'll take my leave.

CLEOPATRA And may, through all the world: 'tis yours, and we,
Your scutcheons and your signs of conquest, shall
Hang in what place you please. Here, my good lord.
                              [*She proffers a scroll.*

CÆSAR   You shall advise me in all for Cleopatra.

CLEOPATRA This is the brief of money, plate and jewels
I am possessed of: 'tis exactly valued,
Not petty things admitted. – Where's Seleucus?

                    Enter SELEUCUS.

SELEUCUS Here, madam.   140

CLEOPATRA This is my treasurer. Let him speak, my lord,
Upon his peril, that I have reserved
To myself nothing. – Speak the truth, Seleucus.

SELEUCUS Madam,
I had rather seal my lips, than to my peril
Speak that which is not.

CLEOPATRA   What have I kept back?

SELEUCUS Enough to purchase what you have made known.

CÆSAR   Nay, blush not, Cleopatra: I approve
Your wisdom in the deed.

CLEOPATRA   See, Cæsar! O, behold,
How pomp is followed! Mine will now be yours,   150
And, should we shift estates, yours would be mine.
The ingratitude of this Seleucus does
Even make me wild. – O slave, of no more trust
Than love that's hired! What, goest thou back?
                                        Thou shalt
Go back, I warrant thee; but I'll catch thine eyes,
Though they had wings. Slave, soulless villain, dog!
O rarely base!

CÆSAR   Good Queen, let us entreat you.

CLEOPATRA O Cæsar, what a wounding shame is this,

That, thou vouchsafing here to visit me,
Doing the honour of thy lordliness   160
To one so meek, that mine own servant should
Parcel the sum of my disgraces by
Addition of his envy![123] Say, good Cæsar,
That I some lady trifles have reserved,
Immoment toys, things of such dignity
As we greet modern friends withal; and say,
Some nobler token I have kept apart
For Livia and Octavia,[124] to induce
Their mediation: must I be unfolded
With one that I have bred? The gods! It smites me   170
Beneath the fall I have. [*To Seleucus:*] Prithee go hence,
Or I shall show the cinders of my spirits
Through th'ashes of my chance. Wert thou a man,
Thou wouldst have mercy on me.

CÆSAR   Forbear, Seleucus.
                                                   [*Exit Seleucus.*

CLEOPATRA Be it known that we, the greatest, are misthought
For things that others do; and when we fall,
We answer others' merits in our name,[125]
Are therefore to be pitied.

CÆSAR   Cleopatra,
Not what you have reserved, nor what acknowledged,
Put we i'th'roll of conquest: still be't yours;   180
Bestow it at your pleasure; and believe
Cæsar's no merchant, to make price with you
Of things that merchants sold. Therefore be cheered;
Make not your thoughts your prisons. No, dear Queen;
For we intend so to dispose you as
Yourself shall give us counsel. Feed, and sleep.
Our care and pity is so much upon you
That we remain your friend; and so, adieu.

CLEOPATRA My master, and my lord!

CÆSAR   Not so. Adieu.
                           [*Flourish. Exeunt Cæsar and his followers.*

CLEOPATRA He words me, girls, he words me, that I should not   190
Be noble to myself: but, hark thee, Charmian.
                                          [*She whispers to Charmian.*

IRAS   Finish, good lady. The bright day is done,
              And we are for the dark.
CLEOPATRA [to Charmian:]   Hie thee again.
              I have spoke already, and it is provided.
              Go put it to the haste.
CHARMIAN   Madam, I will.

                  Enter DOLABELLA.

DOLABELL. Where's the Queen?
CHARMIAN   Behold, sir.   [*Exit Charmian.*
CLEOPATRA   Dolabella?
DOLABELL. Madam, as thereto sworn by your command
              (Which my love makes religion to obey),
              I tell you this: Cæsar through Syria
              Intends his journey, and within three days   200
              You with your children will he send before.
              Make your best use of this; I have performed
              Your pleasure and my promise.
CLEOPATRA   Dolabella,
              I shall remain your debtor.
DOLABELL.   I your servant.
              Adieu, good Queen; I must attend on Cæsar.
CLEOPATRA Farewell, and thanks.   [*Exit Dolabella.*
                          Now, Iras, what think'st thou?
              Thou, an Egyptian puppet, shalt be shown
              In Rome, as well as I: mechanic slaves,
              With greasy aprons, rules and hammers, shall
              Uplift us to the view. In their thick breaths,   210
              Rank of gross diet, shall we be enclouded,
              And forced to drink their vapour.
IRAS   The gods forbid!
CLEOPATRA Nay, 'tis most certain, Iras: saucy lictors
              Will catch at us like strumpets, and scald rhymers
              Ballad us out o'tune. The quick comedians
              Extemporally will stage us, and present
              Our Alexandrian revels: Antony
              Shall be brought drunken forth, and I shall see
              Some squeaking Cleopatra boy my greatness
              I'th'posture of a whore.
IRAS   O the good gods!   220

CLEOPATRA Nay, that's certain.

IRAS   I'll never see't! For I am sure my nails
            Are stronger than mine eyes.

CLEOPATRA   Why, that's the way
            To fool their preparation, and to conquer
            Their most absurd intents.

                    Enter CHARMIAN.

                                    Now, Charmian.
            Show me, my women, like a queen: go fetch
            My best attires. I am again for Cydnus,
            To meet Mark Antony. – Sirrah Iras, go;
            – Now, noble Charmian, we'll dispatch indeed; –
            And when thou hast done this chare I'll give thee leave 230
            To play till Doomsday. Bring our crown and all.
                            [*Exit Iras. Loud voices heard.*
            Wherefore's this noise?

                    Enter a GUARD.

GUARD.   Here is a rural fellow
            That will not be denied your Highness' presence.
            He brings you figs.

CLEOPATRA Let him come in.   [*Exit guard.*
                    – What poor an instrument
            May do a noble deed! He brings me liberty.
            My resolution's placed, and I have nothing
            Of woman in me: now from head to foot
            I am marble-constant; now the fleeting moon
            No planet is of mine.

        Enter the GUARD *with a* CLOWN *(who carries a basket).*

GUARD   This is the man.   240

CLEOPATRA Avoid, and leave him.   [*Exit guard.*
            [*To clown:*] Hast thou the pretty worm of Nilus there,
            That kills and pains not?

CLOWN   Truly, I have him; but I would not be the party that
            should desire you to touch him, for his biting is immor-
            tal: those that do die of it do seldom or never recover.

CLEOPATRA Remember'st thou any that have died on't?

CLOWN   Very many, men, and women too. I heard of one of
            them no longer than yesterday: a very honest woman,

but something given to lie, as a woman should not do   250
but in the way of honesty; how she died of the biting of
it, what pain she felt. Truly, she makes a very good
report o'th'worm;[126] but he that will believe all that they
say, shall never be saved by half that they do; but this is
most falliable: the worm's an odd worm.

CLEOPATRA   Get thee hence; farewell.

CLOWN   I wish you all joy of the worm. [*He puts down the basket.*

CLEOPATRA   Farewell.

CLOWN   You must think this, look you, that the worm will do
his kind.   260

CLEOPATRA   Ay, ay; farewell.

CLOWN   Look you, the worm is not to be trusted but in the
keeping of wise people; for indeed, there is no goodness
in the worm.

CLEOPATRA   Take thou no care; it shall be heeded.

CLOWN   Very good. Give it nothing, I pray you, for it is not
worth the feeding.

CLEOPATRA   Will it eat me?

CLOWN   You must not think I am so simple but I know the devil
himself will not eat a woman: I know that a woman is a   270
dish for the gods, if the devil dress her not. But truly,
these same whoreson devils do the gods great harm in
their women; for in every ten that they make, the devils
mar five.

CLEOPATRA   Well, get thee gone; farewell.

CLOWN   Yes, forsooth. I wish you joy o'th'worm.   [*Exit clown.*

Enter IRAS *with royal regalia.*

CLEOPATRA   Give me my robe, put on my crown: I have
Immortal longings in me. Now no more
The juice of Egypt's grape shall moist this lip.
Yare, yare, good Iras; quick. Methinks I hear   280
Antony call; I see him rouse himself
To praise my noble act. I hear him mock
The luck of Cæsar, which the gods give men
To excuse their after wrath. Husband, I come:
Now to that name my courage prove my title!
I am fire and air; my other elements

I give to baser life. So, have you done?
Come then, and take the last warmth of my lips.
Farewell, kind Charmian. Iras, long farewell.

[*She kisses them. Iras falls and dies.*

Have I the aspic in my lips? Dost fall? 290
If thou and nature can so gently part,
The stroke of death is as a lover's pinch,
Which hurts, and is desired. Dost thou lie still?
If thus thou vanishest, thou tell'st the world
It is not worth leave-taking.

CHARMIAN Dissolve, thick cloud, and rain, that I may say
The gods themselves do weep!

CLEOPATRA   This proves me base:
If she first meet the curlèd Antony,
He'll make demand of her, and spend that kiss
Which is my heaven to have.

[*She takes an asp and applies it to her breast.*

                          Come, thou mortal wretch, 300
With thy sharp teeth this knot intrinsicate
Of life at once untie: poor venomous fool,
Be angry, and dispatch. O, couldst thou speak,
That I might hear thee call great Cæsar 'Ass',
Unpolicied!

CHARMIAN   O Eastern Star!

CLEOPATRA   Peace, peace:
Dost thou not see my baby at my breast,
That sucks the nurse asleep?

CHARMIAN   O break! O break!

CLEOPATRA As sweet as balm, as soft as air, as gentle.
O Antony! – Nay, I will take thee too:

[*She takes a second asp and applies it to her arm.*

What should I stay . . .   [*She dies.* 310

CHARMIAN In this wild world?[127] So, fare thee well.
Now boast thee, Death, in thy possession lies
A lass unparalleled. [*She closes Cleopatra's eyes.*]
                          Downy windows, close;
And golden Phœbus never be beheld
Of eyes again so royal! Your crown's awry:
I'll mend it, and then play.

Enter GUARDS *hastily.*[128]

GUARD 1   Where's the Queen?
CHARMIAN   Speak softly; wake her not.
GUARD 1   Cæsar hath sent –
CHARMIAN   Too slow a messenger.
                                        [*She applies an asp.*
          O come apace, dispatch; I partly feel thee.
GUARD 1   Approach ho! All's not well: Cæsar's beguiled.   320
GUARD 2   There's Dolabella sent from Cæsar: call him.
GUARD 1   What work is here, Charmian? Is this well done?
CHARMIAN It is well done, and fitting for a princess
          Descended of so many royal kings.
          Ah, soldier . . .   [*Charmian dies.*

                Enter DOLABELLA.

DOLABELL. How goes it here?
GUARD 2   All dead.
DOLABELL.   Cæsar, thy thoughts
          Touch their effects in this: thyself art coming
          To see performed the dreaded act which thou
          So sought'st to hinder.
SHOUTS HEARD   A way there, a way for Cæsar!

Enter CÆSAR *and all his* RETINUE, *marching. They halt.*

DOLABELL. O sir, you are too sure an augurer: 330
          That you did fear is done.
CÆSAR   Bravest at the last,
          She levelled at our purposes, and, being royal,
          Took her own way. The manner of their deaths?
          I do not see them bleed.
DOLABELL. [*to Guard 1:*]   Who was last with them?
GUARD 1   A simple countryman, that brought her figs:
          This was his basket.
CÆSAR   Poisoned then.
GUARD 1   O Cæsar,
          This Charmian lived but now; she stood and spake.
          I found her trimming up the diadem
          On her dead mistress; tremblingly she stood,
          And on the sudden dropped.
CÆSAR   O noble weakness!   340

If they had swallowed poison, 'twould appear
By external swelling; but she looks like sleep,
As she would catch another Antony
In her strong toil of grace.[129]

DOLABELL.   Here, on her breast,
There is a vent of blood, and something blown;
The like is on her arm.

GUARD 1   This is an aspic's trail; and these fig-leaves
Have slime upon them, such as th'aspic leaves
Upon the caves of Nile.

CÆSAR   Most probable
That so she died; for her physician tells me   350
She hath pursued conclusions infinite
Of easy ways to die. Take up her bed,
And bear her women from the monument.
She shall be buried by her Antony.
No grave upon the earth shall clip in it
A pair so famous. High events as these
Strike those that make them; and their story is
No less in pity, than his glory which
Brought them to be lamented.[130] Our army shall
In solemn show attend this funeral;   360
And then to Rome. Come, Dolabella, see
High order in this great solemnity.   [*Exeunt.*

FINIS.

NOTES ON *ANTONY AND CLEOPATRA*

In these notes, the abbreviations include the following:

cf.:   *confer* (Latin): compare;

e.g.:   *exempli gratia* (Latin): for example;

F1:   the First Folio (1623);

F2:   the Second Folio (1632);

i.e.:   *id est* (Latin): that is;

Plutarch: *The Lives of the Noble Grecians and Romanes*, translated by Sir Thomas North (London: T. Vautroullier and J. Wight, 1579);

S.D.:   stage-direction;

sic: (Latin): thus; so it appears;

S.P.:   speech-prefix.

In the case of a pun or an ambiguity, the meanings are distinguished as (a) and (b), or as (a), (b) and (c), etc. Biblical quotations are taken from the Geneva Bible, though I modernise the spelling, as in the case of quotations from Plutarch.

1 (title) *ANTONY AND CLEOPATRA*: The title in F1 is: 'THE TRAGEDIE OF Anthonie, and Cleopatra.' [*sic*].

2 (1.1.6) *tawny front*.: brown face (with pun on 'front' as 'battle-line').

3 (1.1.12) *triple pillar of the world*: Antony, Octavius Cæsar and Lepidus were then the three rulers (Triumvirs) of the vast Roman Empire.

4 (1.1.16–17) *I'll . . . earth*.: Cleopatra means: 'I'll set a boundary to the extent of your love: define that extent.' Antony's reply alludes anachronistically to Revelation 21:1: 'I saw a new heaven, & a new earth . . . ' (The play's opening is set in 40 B.C.)

5 (1.1.31–2) *else . . . scolds*.: 'or else that's how you blush when shrill-tongued Fulvia (your wife) scolds you.'

6 (1.1.38–40) *in which . . . peerless.*: 'a matter in which I command the world, under penalty of punishment, to recognise that we stand unrivalled.'

7 (1.1.43) *Will be himself.*: (a) 'will remain the fool that he is.'; (b) 'will remain singular.'.

8 (1.2.4) *which . . . garlands!*: 'who, you say, is bound (if he is *my* husband) to be the champion cuckold of Egypt, loading his horns (the sign of a cuckold) with the garlands denoting a victor!'. (F1's 'change' is often emended as 'charge'.)

9 (1.2.15–17) *You . . . old.*: The soothsayer means that she will be nobler, more beautiful in character (which is true of her eventual conduct: see Act 5, scene 2). Charmian takes him to mean that she will become physically more beautiful (and perhaps lighter in complexion). Iras says that Charmian will, on the contrary, grow old and resort to cosmetics.

10 (1.2.22) *I had . . . drinking.*: The liver was regarded as the source of the passions. She means: 'I would rather have my liver inflamed by alcohol than by unrequited passion.'

11 (1.2.26–7) *a child . . . homage.*: This is another anachronistic reference. She would like her child to elicit the homage of Herod the Great, the king who (according to Matthew 2:16) killed all the infants in and around Bethlehem. Her 'three kings' may recall those who paid homage to Jesus.

12 (1.2.37) *Out . . . witch.*: probably: 'Wrong, you buffoon! I'll exonerate you from the charge of having supernatural powers (as your prognostications are ridiculous).'

13 (1.2.45) *E'en as . . . famine.*: The river Nile's regular flooding made its valley fertile.

14 (1.2.73) *Here . . . Antony.*: Enobarbus is probably being sarcastic, implying that Cleopatra rules Antony.

15 (1.2.95–9) *Labienus. . .Ionia,*: Quintus Labienus, foe of Antony and Octavius, led an army of Parthians which conquered Roman provinces in the Middle East. (Line 97 is regular if 'Asia' is pronounced trisyllabically and 'Euphrates' is accented, as indicated, on syllables one and three.)

16 (1.2.108–15) *At . . . Sicyon.*: I follow F1 more closely here than do some editors who try to simplify this awkward sequence of messengers.

17 (1.2.120–22) *The present . . . itself::* 'Just as a wheel turns, so what is a pleasure to us at present becomes displeasure later:'.

18 (1.2.146–7) *she . . . Jove.*: Jove (Jupiter, the supreme god) was

sometimes termed in Latin *Iuppiter pluvialis*: 'Jupiter the rain-giver'.

19 (1.2.159) *shows . . . earth,*: 'reveals to man that the gods are tailors to the world;'.

20 (1.2.160–63) *when . . . lamented.*: obscene punning. 'Robes' could mean 'loose women', while 'members' could mean 'people', 'limbs' and 'male sexual organs'; 'cut' means 'wound' and 'slash in a garment' here, but it could also mean 'vulva'; and 'case' here means 'situation', 'clothing' and 'vagina'.

21 (1.2.169–70) *especially . . . abode.*: (a) 'especially Cleopatra's business, which wholly depends on your residing here.'; (b) 'especially Cleopatra's vagina, which, hole-like, depends on being filled by you.'.

22 (1.2.182–4) *begin . . . son,*: 'begin to bestow the title and honours due to Pompey the Great upon his younger son, Sextus,'. Pompey the Great was the defeated rival of Julius Cæsar, who had adopted his great-nephew, Octavius, as his heir.

23 (1.2.185–7) *stands . . . danger.*: 'is a contender for the title of supreme warrior; and his power, if it continues, may imperil the [Roman] world from east to west'.

24 (1.2.188–9) *like . . . poison.*: It was sometimes believed that if a horse-hair were left in water, it would turn into a snake.

25 (1.3.40–41) *I would . . . Egypt.*: 'I wish I were a big man, as you are. Then you would know what courage [to resist your departure] the Queen of Egypt possessed.'

26 (1.3.84–5) *How . . . chafe.*: 'how well this Roman, in enacting his fury, emulates the mighty Hercules [supposedly his ancestor], who went mad.'

27 (1.3.90–91) *my oblivion . . . forgotten.*: 'my memory is so prone to forgetfulness that it is just like Antony, who readily forgets me.'

28 (1.3.93–5) *'Tis . . . this.*: 'By "idleness" you mean "folly and frivolity". It can also mean "neglect of labour"; but my folly is tantamount to very hard work (even the labour of childbirth), when it is of heartfelt concern to me.'

29 (1.4.6) *the Queen of Ptolemy*: Cleopatra had been married to one of her brothers, Ptolemy XIII, and, after his death in battle against Julius Cæsar, to another brother, Ptolemy XIV, whom she allegedly poisoned. (These Ptolemies have sometimes been numbered XII and XIII respectively.)

30 (1.4.24–5) *No way . . . lightness.*: 'by no means excuse his faults, when his levity is so burdensome to us.'

31 (1.4.25–30) *If . . . chid*: 'If he simply filled his leisure-time with
sensual pleasures, he would be punished by nauseous excess and
venereal disease; but to waste the pressing time, when he is being
summoned from his amusements and called by his own responsi-
bilities as well as ours, deserves to be reprimanded'.

32 (1.4.41–4) *It . . . lacked.*: 'from the earliest state of society, the
lesson has been repeated: the man who is in power has been
popular only until he gained power, while the man who is out of
favour (and is never loved until he is unworthy of love) becomes
valued because people miss him.'

33 (1.4.55) *Than . . . resisted.*: 'than his forces could if confronted in
battle.'

34 (1.5.19) *What . . . Mars.*: Venus, beautiful wife of the blacksmith
Vulcan, copulated with the heroic Mars.

35 (1.5.24–5) *demi-Atlas . . . men.*: Atlas carried the world on his
shoulders. Antony is 'half' an Atlas because he and Octavius Cæsar
share control of the Roman empire. Here, 'arm and burgonet' (i.e.
strong arm and efficient helmet) is a synecdoche for 'warrior and
defender'.

36 (1.5.29) *That . . . black,*: 'whose skin has been darkened by the
sun, as if Phœbus Apollo, the sun-god, were a lover who had
bruised me with his erotic pinches,'.

37 (1.5.30–35) *Cæsar . . . Pompey . . . life.*: One of her former lovers
was Julius Cæsar. Another was Gnæus Pompeius, elder son of
Pompey the Great; but Shakespeare's phrase 'great Pompey' gives
the impression that she was loved by his famous father. (Sextus
Pompeius, younger son of Pompey the Great, appears in Act 2.)

38 (2.1, S.D.) *Enter . . . manner'.*: F1 has '*Enter Pompey, Menecrates,
and Menas, in warlike manner.*' In this scene, its speech-prefixes,
other than for Pompey and Varrius, are always '*Mene*'. Clearly,
one of the speakers must be Menas, for he is addressed as such by
Pompey; and in F1's Act 2, sc. 7, '*Menas*' is spelt '*Menes*'. Some
editors therefore conclude that in Act 2, sc. 1, the S.P. '*Mene.*'
should always represent '*Menas*'. Other editors, noting the different tone of the first two '*Mene.*' speeches, ascribe those to
Menecrates.

39 (2.1.51–2) *it . . . hands.*: 'our lives depend entirely on fighting as
strongly as we can.'

40 (2.2.7–8) *Were . . . today.*: Jerking a man's beard was an insult, so
Enobarbus wants Antony to give Octavius the opportunity to
provoke a quarrel.

41 (2.2.26–8) *Nor . . . thus.*: 'Nor curstness grow to th'matter' means 'and do not add rancour to the argument'. Antony's 'do thus' may mean 'speak mildly' or may indicate a conciliating action, e.g. embracing Octavius or Lepidus.

42 (2.2.50–59) *You do . . . this.*: Antony says that his brother never cited him as the pretext for his action; furthermore, he has learnt this from reliable informants ('true reports') who had fought alongside Octavius Cæsar. Antony had no appetite ('stomach') for such wars. Finally, he says, 'if you want to patch together a quarrel and present it as though it were a whole substantial case, you can't use this stuff '.

43 (2.2.62–3) *I know . . . thought,*: 'I am certain – I know you could not fail to be compelled to acknowledge,'.

44 (2.2.118–19) *our conditions . . . acts.*: 'our dispositions producing such conflicting actions.'

45 (2.2.123–4) *Thou . . . Octavia.*: Of Octavius Cæsar's two sisters called 'Octavia', Antony married the younger, Octavius's full sister. She was not a half-sister 'by the mother's side'.

46 (2.2.212–13) *tended . . . adornings.*: 'waited in her sight, and their curving movements formed embellishments.' (The Nereides were beautiful sea–nymphs, daughters of the sea–god Nereus.)

47 (2.2.221–3) *which . . . nature.*: 'which, but for the fact that nature abhors a vacuum, would also have gone to gaze at Cleopatra, thus making a gap in the natural realm.'

48 (2.2.230–31) *And . . . only.*: 'and, for this public meal, paid with his heart, even though (instead of eating the food) he only consumed her with his gaze.'

49 (2.2.233) *He . . . cropped.*: Julius Cæsar was probably the father of Cleopatra's son Cæsarion ('Little Cæsar', here the 'crop').

50 (2.3.37–8) *When . . . odds.*: 'when the odds in my favour are everything against nothing, and, against all odds, his quails always beat mine in the quail-fighting ring.'

51 (2.5.23) *his sword Philippan.*: This was the sword that Antony had wielded at the battle of Philippi when he defeated Brutus and Cassius, the assassins of Julius Cæsar.

52 (2.5.40–41) *Thou . . . man.*: The classical Furies or Erinyes, female spirits of revenge, bore snakes instead of hair. (Here 'formal' means 'sane and normal'.)

53 (2.5.103) *That . . . sure of!*: perhaps: 'who are not married, though you are sure of a marriage!', or 'who are not hateful, as is your knowledge!'. (Some editors emend F1's 'art' as 'act'.)

54 (2.5.116–17) *Though . . . Mars.*: 'though he be depicted from one aspect as an ugly monster (a snake-haired Gorgon, like Medusa, whose stare turned men to stone), from another aspect he's a divine war-lord (like Mars, the god of war).' Some pictures offered one image when upright and a contrasting image when inverted.

55 (2.6.10–19) *I do . . . man?*: Pompey's point is that just as Julius Cæsar (murdered by Brutus, Cassius and others in the Capitol at Rome) found avengers in Antony and Octavius, so Pompey's father, Pompey the Great, should find avengers in his son and the son's allies. Cæsar's ghost appeared to Brutus on the eve of the battle of Philippi, where Brutus and Cassius died. Pompey the Great, defeated by Julius Cæsar, had fled to Egypt but was assassinated there by order of Ptolemy XIII (Cleopatra's brother) or his ministers. Pompey Junior is naturally sympathetic to Brutus and Cassius, the republican conspirators against Julius Cæsar, and antipathetic to those who vanquished them. Here he depicts himself as a republican who, like the conspirators, wants a man to be only a man and not a king or god.

56 (2.6.22–3) *th'ingratitude . . . father.*: He cites Rome's ingratitude in acclaiming Julius Cæsar's victories over Pompey the Great (who had served the city well as a general) and his sons. In *Julius Cæsar*, Act 1, scene 1, two Roman tribunes denounce the rejoicing plebeians for their 'ingratitude' to Pompey.

57 (2.6.27–9) *Thou . . . mayst.*: Plutarch says that Antony acquired the house of Pompey the Great in 'open sale', but then declined to pay for it. Antony resembles the cuckoo, which makes use of another bird's nest.

59 (2.6.44–6) *When . . . friendly.*: According to Plutarch, Pompey had indeed been hospitable to Antony's mother and Fulvia when they had fled to Sicily.

58 (2.6.68–70) *Apollodorus . . . mattress.*: Plutarch says that Cleopatra's sexual relationship with Julius Cæsar began when he summoned her and she concealed herself in 'a mattress or flockbed' so that Apollodorus could smuggle her into Cæsar's castle at Alexandria.

60 (2.6.94–6) *There . . . kissing.*: Here, 'land service' means both 'military service' and 'thieving'; and the 'two thieves kissing' are their hands clasping.

61 (2.7.4–5) *They have . . . disposition,*: Probably, others have obliged Lepidus to drink as an act of charity (to aid reconciliation). The obscure phrase 'pinch one another by the disposition' may mean: (a)

'the political arrangement they have made proves galling to each of them'; or (b) 'they irritate each other in accordance with their differing temperaments'. (Lepidus's speeches will contain plenty of sibilants to be slurred drunkenly.)

62 (2.7.13–15) *To . . . cheeks.*: 'To be placed in a high circle in which nobody can see you doing anything is like having empty sockets without eyeballs in them, which sadly mars the cheeks.' (Planets and stars were supposed to be set in crystalline spheres. Punningly, 'disaster' can mean 'deprive of stars or planets' as well as 'ill-star, blight or mar'.)

63 (2.7.96–7) *Be . . . answer;*: 'Adapt to the situation.' 'I'll reply, "It's better to master it";'. (He could 'master it' either by abstaining or, as later lines suggest, by drinking more.)

64 (3.1.1–5) *Now . . . Crassus.*: Marcus Crassus, an ally of Julius Cæsar, had been defeated by the Parthians and treacherously killed by Orodes, the Parthian king. Now Ventidius has avenged him by routing the Parthians; furthermore Pacorus, son of Orodes, has been slain. The phrase 'darting Parthia' means 'Parthia, land of javelin-throwing warriors'. (The Parthian empire included the region later known as Iraq.)

65 (3.1.28–30) *Thou hast . . . distinction.*: 'You, Ventidius, have discretion, without which hardly any difference can be discerned between a soldier and his sword.'

66 (3.2.20) *They . . . beetle.*: either (a) 'They are the lumps of dung on which he, the beetle, feeds.', or (b) 'They are his scaly wings, and he the beetle who depends on them for flight.' (The latter reading, though disputed, gains support from *Macbeth*, Act 3, scene 2. The meanings of 'shard' included 'scale'.)

67 (3.2.26–7) *as my farthest . . . approof.*: 'as my utmost pledge will testify to your demonstrable worthiness.'

68 (3.2.51–2) *He has . . . horse;*: Agrippa means that Cæsar certainly looks as though he might shed tears (as a cloud sheds rain). Enobarbus recalls that a 'clouded' horse is supposedly one which, having a partly or totally dark face, is deemed unreliable or vicious.

69 (3.2.57–9) *That...too:* 'True enough: that year he suffered from catarrh [so that his eyes ran]. What he wilfully destroyed, he mourned so much – believe me! – that I wept too.'

70 (3.3.3–5) *Herod . . . have;*: Herod the Great was King of the Jews at this time. He was sometimes confused with his son, Herod Antipas, who presented John the Baptist's head to Salome.

71 (3.3.28) *And I . . . thirty.*: Commentators' estimates of Cleopatra's
age at that time vary between 28 (John Wilders) and 38 (Michael
Neill). Although, historically, the lower estimate is probable,
Shakespeare (while compressing the time-scale) depicts her as
clearly past 30 and approaching middle age. (At her death, she was
38 or 39.)

72 (3.5.17–18) *his officer . . . Pompey.*: Plutarch says that Pompey, after
being defeated in Sicily, went to Samos and was there killed on
Antony's orders by Antony's lieutenant. Shakespeare's modifica-
tion makes Antony seem less Machiavellian.

73 (3.6.6–8) *Cæsarion . . . them.*: In addition to Cæsarion, her son
supposedly by Julius Cæsar, Cleopatra had two sons and a
daughter by Antony: Alexander Helios (i.e. Sun), Ptolemy Phila-
delphus and Cleopatra Selene (i.e. Moon).

74 (3.6.52–3) *The ostentation . . . unloved.*: 'the display of my love; and, if
love is not so demonstrated, it is shunned and denied love in return.'

75 (3.6.61) *Being . . . him.*: either: (a) 'her return curtailing the gap
between him and his lustful pleasure (with Cleopatra).'; or (b,
emending 'abstract' as 'obstruct'): 'she being an obstruction
between him and lustful pleasure.'.

76 (3.6.87–9) *the high . . . you.*: In line 88, the phrase 'makes his
ministers' follows F1. F2 has 'make his ministers'. Some editors
emend the phrase as 'make their ministers' or 'make them
ministers'. (Line 78's 'does' follows F1; F2 has 'doe'.)

77 (3.6.95–6) *gives . . . us.*: 'gives his powerful authority to a whore
who loudly denounces us.'

78 (3.7.5–6) *Is't . . . person?*: The sense here is: 'Hasn't war been
declared against me? Why shouldn't I be personally present?'.
(Editors variously emend F1's 'If not, denounc'd against vs, why
should not we be there in person.'.)

79 (3.7.60) *Thetis!*: Thetis was a sea-goddess and mother of the
warrior Achilles.

80 (3.7.68–9) *his whole...on't::* 'his whole plan of action does not
proceed from a real source of strength:'.

81 (3.7.80–81) *With . . . some.*: 'The present time is like a woman in
labour: it is burdened with news, and every minute yields some.'
(F1's 'with labour' is often emended as 'in labour'.)

82 (3.10.10) *ribaudred . . . Egypt*: F1's 'ribaudred' may mean 'debauched'. It has been variously emended: e.g., as 'ribald-rid'
('ridden by – or familiar to – a ribald man or ribald men'),
'ribanded' ('decked with ribbons') and 'riband-red'.

83　(3.11.35–40) *He . . . war.*:　In lines 35 and 38, 'He' refers to Octavius Cæsar, who, Antony says, depended on subordinates ('dealt on lieutenantry'). When defeated by the forces of Antony and Octavius, Brutus committed suicide. Cassius's death was aided by Titinius.

84　(3.11.72) *our schoolmaster,*:　the tutor of the offspring of Cleopatra's union with Antony.

85　(3.12.29–33) *Women . . . law.*:　'Even when women enjoy good fortune they are not resolute, and neediness will make the purest vestal virgin break her vows of chastity. Exploit your cunning, Thidias. Personally decree the reward for your endeavours, and Cæsar will pay it as if bound by law.'

86　(3.13.26) *lay . . . apart,*:　This could mean (a) 'suspend his fine advantages'; (b) 'put aside his showy counterparts to my forces'; or (c) 'put away his showy insults'. Some editors emend F1's 'comparisons' as 'caparisons' (i.e. 'trappings').

87　(3.13.53–5) *Cæsar . . . Cæsar.*:　'Cæsar begs you not to consider your wretched situation except as an opportunity for Cæsar.' (He implies that she may expect magnanimity.)

88　(3.13.118) *Gnæus Pompey's,*:　He should be referring to the son of Pompey the Great and elder brother of this play's Pompey, though Shakespeare may have confused him with his father, whose full name was the same: Gnæus (or Cneius) Pompeius Magnus.

89　(3.13.126–8) *O . . . herd!*:　Psalm 68:15 says that Bashan (Basan) is a high mountain; Psalm 22:12–13 says that it produces bulls which 'gape . . . *as* a ramping and roaring lion'. Antony means that he is a champion cuckold (deceived man bearing horns) and in his rage could out-roar the bulls.

90　(4.3, S.D.) Enter . . . SOLDIERS.:　F1's S.D. is '*Enter a Company of Soldiours.*', and the subsequent directions in F1 are '*They meete other Soldiers.*' and '*They place themselues in euery corner of the Stage.*'. The dialogue requires only four soldiers.

91　(4.3.12, S.D.) *Music . . . beneath.*:　F1's S.D. is '*Musicke of the Hoboyes is vnder the Stage.*'. 'Hoboyes' (or 'hautboys': probably plural, possibly singular) refers to an early form of oboe.

92　(4.4.8) *Sooth . . . be.*:　'Truly, indeed, I'll help. This is how it must fit.' F1's interjection 'law' ('indeed') is sometimes emended as 'la', though in *Love's Labour's Lost* it rhymes with 'flaw'.

93　(4.5, S.D.) *a SOLDIER . . . them.*:　This is evidently the 'worthy soldier' who advised Antony previously (Act 3, scene 7).

94 (4.6.6–7) *the three-nooked ... freely.*: probably (following Plutarch): 'the three main divisions of the world – Europe, Asia and Africa – will then enjoy peace.' (Alternatively, the three nooks may be Rome, Athens and Alexandria.)

95 (4.6.12–16) *Alexas ... him.*: Plutarch says that Alexas, sent to Herod by Antony, betrayed Antony by persuading Herod to serve Octavius Cæsar; but Octavius then sentenced Alexas to death.

96 (4.7.7–8) *I had ... 'H'.*: Another cut has converted the scar from a T-shape to an H-shape, and it aches. (The noun 'ache' was then pronounced 'aitch'.)

97 (4.8.6–7) *Not ... Hectors.*: 'not as if you were servants of the campaign, but as if you identified yourselves with me; and you have all revealed yourselves to be as brave as the legendary Hector of Troy.'

98 (4.10.1–3) *Their ... air;*: The four essential elements were deemed to be earth, water, fire and air: Antony says he would be willing to fight Octavius in any of them. In line 3, as often in Shakespeare, 'fire' is disyllabic ('*fi*-er'): cf. 'hired' ('*hi*-erd') at 5.1.21.

99 (4.12.3–4) *Swallows ... nests.*: In Plutarch's account, swallows nested in Cleopatra's flagship but were driven away by others which pulled their nests down: 'a marvellous ill sign'.

100 (4.12.9, S.D.) *Alarum ... ends.*: At what is now the start of scene 12, F1 has the following direction: '*Alarum afarre off, as at a Sea-fight.*' Since Antony then says 'Yet they are not joined' (i.e. 'They haven't started the battle yet'), various editors move the direction to a later point. (One editor's conjecture that F1's S.D. refers to preparations only is unsatisfactory, for it leaves no direction for the battle itself.) I have adapted the S.D. to make clear that battle is both joined and concluded, as Antony's words in lines 9–13 show.

101 (4.12.20–24) *The hearts ... am.*: These lines exemplify a famous recurrent image-cluster in which Shakespeare associates fickle followers with pet dogs and melting sweets. (See Caroline Spurgeon's *Shakespeare's Imagery*.) The verb 'barked' means 'fatally stripped of its bark' and was perhaps evoked by association with barking dogs.

102 (4.12.37) *For poor'st diminutives, for dolts,*: 'instead of the poorest dwarves and idiots'.

103 (4.12.43–7) *The shirt ... self.*: In *Metamorphoses*, Ovid gives the following version of the Nessus story. Nessus was a centaur who attempted to rape Hercules' wife, Deianira. Hercules (also called Alcides) then shot him with a poisoned arrow. Dying, Nessus

gave to Deianira a shirt anointed with his poisoned blood, telling her that it would act as a love-charm. Some time afterwards, fearing Hercules' infidelity, she sent him the shirt; but, when Hercules wore it, the poison caused him terrible agonies. Having furiously hurled the shirt's bringer, Lichas, high in the air so that he fell into the sea, Hercules finally committed himself to the flames of a pyre. (Traditionally, pictures of Hercules show him holding a massive club.)

104 (4.13.1–3) *O, he's . . . embossed.*: Telamonian Ajax ('Telamon'), the Greek warrior, competed with Ulysses for the armour and shield of Achilles. Defeated in the contest, Ajax went mad and killed himself. The ferocious 'Boar of Thessaly' was sent by the goddess Diana to ravage Calydon, a region of Thessalia (Thessaly) in eastern Greece. 'Embossed' means 'frenzied, frothing and sweaty'.

105 (4.14.19–20) *Packed . . . triumph.*: 'arranged the cards in Cæsar's favour, and treacherously gambled my glory away so that an enemy can play a trump-card and triumph.' ('Trump' derives from 'triumph'.)

106 (4.14.39–40) *The seven-fold . . . heart.*: 'Even the shield of the warrior Ajax, which was made of brass and seven layers of oxhide, could not protect my heart from this series of blows.'

107 (4.14.52–5) *Where . . . ours.*: 'In Elysium (the blissful region of the classical underworld), where the souls of the dead recline on beds of flowers, we'll walk hand in hand; and, by our high-spirited bearing [*or* our bearing as ghosts], we'll make the other ghosts gaze in admiration, so that Dido and Æneas will lose their followers, and we'll dominate the entire area.' Dido was deserted by her lover, Æneas, and (according to Virgil's *Æneid*) shunned him in the underworld; but Antony implies that they were reunited there. 'Sprightly' suggests 'spritely' ('like spirits'), and 'haunt' means 'resort' but also suggests 'place haunted by ghosts'.

108 (4.14.74–8) *with pleached . . . ensued.*: 'with folded arms, bending down his neck to submit to punishment, his face inured to deep disgrace; while the chariot of lucky Cæsar, drawn ahead of Antony, marked out by contrast, as clearly as with a branding-iron, the abjection of that man following?'

109 (4.14.105, S.D.) DERCETUS: F1 offers editors the choice of 'Decretas' or 'Dercetus'. North's Plutarch offers 'Dercetæus'.

110 (4.15.43–5) *let . . . offence.*: 'let me complain so loudly that

Fortune (that false hussy) will break her wheel because she will be so offended by me.' Fortune, goddess of chance, turned her wheel to influence human lives.

111 (5.1.2–3) *Being . . . makes.*: 'Tell him that, being thus defeated, his delays (in surrendering) are a mere self-mockery.'

112 (5.1.45–8) *the heart . . . this.*: 'the heart which inspired mine with aspirations: that our guiding stars, irreconcilable, should reduce our equality to this disparity.'

113 (5.1.59–60) *Cæsar . . . ungentle.*: 'Cæsar cannot incline to be unkind.' Editors emend F1's 'leaue' in various ways: e.g. as 'lean' (here), 'live' and 'learn'.

114 (5.2.7–8) *Which sleeps . . . Cæsar's.*: 'which induces a sleep in which we never again experience this dungy earth, which nurtures beggars and Cæsars alike.' This reading is supported by 1.1.35–6. Some editors emend F1's 'dung' as 'dug' ('breast or nipple, often an animal's'), which is supported by the reference to the 'nurse' and by 5.2.306–7.

115 (5.2.27) *that will . . . kindness,*: 'who will beg you to help him to be kind to you,'.

116 (5.2, S.D. after 34) *Inside . . . approach.*: Plutarch says that three Romans entered the monument by means of a ladder to the high window through which Antony had been hauled.

117 (5.2.50–51) *If . . . neither.*: 'and, if trivial chattering will, for once, be necessary [in keeping me awake], I will not sleep either.'

118 (5.2.60–62) *rather . . . chains!*: A gibbet (or gallows) was used to expose the corpse of an executed person. Shakespeare envisaged an Egyptian pyramid as a column or obelisk. In line 61, 'pyramides' has four syllables, being accentuated on the second.

119 (5.2.81) *The little . . . earth.*: F1 has 'The little o'th'earth.', which could mean 'the inferior people of the world.', but editors usually emend it as 'The little O, the earth.' (meaning 'the little circle, the earth's sphere.') or 'The little O o'th'earth.'.

120 (5.2.83–4) *propertied . . . spheres,*: 'as musical in quality as the harmonious heavenly spheres in which the planets and stars are fixed,'.

121 (5.2.87–92) *an autumn . . . pocket.*: F1's '*Anthony* it was' is usually emended as 'autumn 'twas'. After 'reaping.', the meaning is: 'Just as a dolphin shows its back above the ocean, so Antony was never submerged by the pleasures which were his natural element. His servants (in livery, i.e. uniform,) included king and princes; and he gave away realms and islands as if they were merely silver coins

("plates") fallen from his pocket.'

122 (5.2.97–100) *Nature . . . quite.*: 'Nature lacks sufficient material to rival the strange shapes that Fancy can create; yet to imagine an Antony (who really existed) means that Nature has produced a masterpiece to oppose Fancy and condemn to insignificance all fanciful images.'

123 (5.2.162–3) *Parcel . . . envy!*: perhaps: 'complete the sum of my disgraces by adding his envy!'.

124 (5.2.168) *Livia and Octavia,*: Octavius Cæsar's wife and sister.

125 (5.2.177) *We . . . name,*: The sense is either (a) 'we are personally held accountable for other people's misdeeds;', or (b) 'we are held accountable for other people's misdeeds committed in our name;'.

126 (5.2.250–53) *but something . . . worm;*: The rural fellow ('Clowne' in F1) uses 'lie' to mean 'tell a lie' and 'lie in bed with a man', 'the worm' to mean 'the asp' and 'the penis', and 'died' to mean not only 'experienced death' but also 'had an orgasm'.

127 (5.2.311) *wild world?*: F1 has 'wilde World?'. Some editors emend this as 'vile world?'. The former, meaning 'world of turmoil and ferocity', contrasts well with Cleopatra's sense of a 'gentle' death; the latter fits her sense of transcending a base world.

128 (5.2, S.D. after 316) *Enter . . . hastily.*: F1's S.D. is: '*Enter the Guard rustling in, and Dolabella.*' Here, '*rustling*' perhaps means '*clattering*': haste is implied. A few lines later, F1 specifies a different entry for Dolabella.

129 (5.2.344) *her strong toil of grace.*: 'the strong net of her gracious charms.'

130 (5.2.357–9) *their story . . . lamented.*: 'their story is no less worthy of pity than I (who brought them to their lamentable end) am worthy of glory.'

GLOSSARY

Where a pun or an ambiguity occurs, the meanings are distinguished as (a) and (b), or (a), (b) and (c), etc. Otherwise, alternative meanings are distinguished as (i) and (ii), or as (i), (ii) and (iii), etc. Abbreviations include the following: adj., adjective; adv., adverb; e.g., for example; n., noun; *O.E.D.*, *Oxford English Dictionary*; per.: perhaps; pd., pronounced; vb., verb.

A, a (pronoun): 2.7.87; 3.11.72; 3.13.132: he.

abode: stay.

absolute: (i: 1.2.2; 3.7.42; 4.14.117:) perfect; (ii: 2.2.169; 4.3.10:) complete.

abstract: (i: 1.4.9:) epitome; (ii: 3.6.61: a) short cut; (b, as 'obstruct':) obstruction.

abuse: (i: 3.6.86; 5.2.43:) misuse; (ii: 3.13.108:) deceive.

abysm: abyss, gulf.

accidents unpurposed: random incidents.

adieu: goodbye.

admiral: flagship.

admire: 3.7.24: wonder at.

admit: 5.2.139: include.

a-ducking: down into the sea.

afeard: afraid.

affect: 1.3.71: be inclined.

affection: passion, desire.

alarum: battle-noises.

Alcides: Hercules, god of physical strength.

allay: 2.5.50: (a) abate; (b) alloy.

all-obeying breath: voice that all obey.

alms-drink: drink on behalf of someone.

angle: fishing-rod.

answer (vb.): (i: 3.12.33: a) obey; (b) effect; (ii: 3.13.27, 36:) meet in combat; (iii: 5.2.177:) pay for; **answering to**: 5.2.102: matching.

antick (vb.): make grotesque.

apart: (i: 3.13.26; 5.2.168:) aside; (ii: 3.13.47:) privately.

appeal (n.): impeachment.

apply: adapt.

appointment: state of equipment.

approof: 3.2.27: (a) trial; (b) proof.

approve: confirm.

Arabian bird: the unique phœnix.

argument: evidence.

arm-gaunt: (per.) battle-worn.

art: magic.

as: (i: 1.2.95; 3.13.85; 4.1.1;

5.2.343:) as if; (ii: 1.4.22:
a) though; (b) however;
(iii: 5.2.20:) that.

aspéct: 1.5.34: (a) look;
(b) glance.

aspic: asp, small cobra.

atone: reconcile.

attend: (i: 2.2.65:) regard;
(ii: 3.10.33:) await.

Avaunt!: Go away!

avoid: withdraw.

Bacchanals: dances for Bacchus.

Bacchus: god of wine.

bade (pd. 'bad'): told.

band: (i: 2.6.116; 3.2.26:) bond,
pledge; (ii: 3.12.25): body of
troops.

banquet: dessert with wine.

battery: 4.14.40: (a) bombard-
ment; (b) knock-out blow.

battle: (i: 3.8.3:) land-fighting;
(ii: 3.9.2:) ships arrayed for
battle.

bear (vb.): (i: 1.3.67:) harbour;
(ii: 2.7.107:) maintain.

beck: beckoning.

becomings: charms.

beggary: poverty.

belike: probably.

bench-hole: latrine-hole.

bent (n.): curve.

betimes: early

blasted: stricken, blighted.

blood: 1.2.185; 1.5.76: spirit,
mettle; **in blood:** 3.13.174:
(a) bloodstained; (b) in full
vigour.

blossoming: flourishing.

blow (vb.): (i: 4.6.34:) distend to
bursting; (ii: 5.2.60:) foul.

blown: (i: 3.13.39:) decayed; (ii:
4.4.25:) played on trumpets;
(iii: 5.2.345:) emitted.

Boar of Thessaly: sent by
Artemis to ravage Calydon.

boggler: 3.13.110: (a) fickle jade;
(b) equivocator.

bolt up: fetter.

bond: duty.

bondman: slave.

boot (n.): advantage.

boot (vb.): compensate.

bound: (i: 2.5.58: a) married;
(b) indebted; (ii: 2.6.112:)
compelled.

boy (vb.): reduce to boyish
mimicry.

branchless: mutilated.

brand (vb.): mark out.

brave (vb.): defy.

brave (adj.): splendid.

break: 1.2.172: disclose;
breaking: 5.1.14: (a) disclosure;
(b) destruction; **breaking
forth:** making war.

breathed: 3.13.178: refreshed.

breeze: 3.10.14: (a) gadfly;
(b) breeze.

brief (n.): summary.

brief (adj.): speedy.

briefly: soon.

broad-fronted: (per.) wide-browed.

brooch (vb.): adorn.

brows' bent: eyebrows' curves.

buffet: stand the buffet: (a) be
jostled; (b) exchange punches.

burgonet: ample helmet.

burthen: burden: load.

but: 3.11.47; 4.11.1: unless.

by: 2.7.5; 3.3.39: according to.

call on: 1.4.28: call to account.

cantle: segment.

cap: hold one's cap off: show
deference.

captain: military leader, senior
officer.

cárbuncled: studded with gems.

carriage: 1.3.85: (a) deportment;
(b) performance.

case: (i: 1.2.162: a) situation;
(b) clothing; (b) vagina;
(ii: 4.14.42; 4.15.89: a)
container; (b) body.

cast: (i: 1.2.134; 2.6.54; 4.12.12:)
throw; (ii: 2.2.218:) send;
(iii: 2.6.23:) laid; (iv: 3.2.17:)
calculate.

censuring: condemning.

chafe: carriage of his chafe:
wielding his anger.

chance (n.): (i: 2.3.35:) luck;
(ii: 3.7.47:) chance; (iii: 3.10.37;
5.2.173:) fortunes; (3.13.81:)
setback; (5.2.119:) accident.

chance (vb.): 3.4.13: occur.

chaps: chops: jaws.   –

chare: chore: menial task.

charge (n.): (i: 3.7.16: a) cost; (b)
responsibility; (ii: 4.4.19:) duty.

charge (vb.) (i: 1.2.4:) load; (ii:
4.5.13; 4.6.8:) order.

charm: (i: 2.1.20: a) spell;
(b) appeal; (ii: 4.12.16, 25:)
enchantress.

check: rebuke.

chuck: chick (affectionate term).

circle: crown.

civil: (i: 1.3.45:) drawn in civil
war; (ii: 5.1.16:) urban.

civilly: politely.

clap: clapped up: confined;
claps on: fits hastily.

clear: innocent.

Cleopatra: 'Glory of the Father'.

clip: (i: 4.8.8:) embrace;
(ii: 5.2.355:) enclose.

close (adv.): 4.9.6: hidden.

cloth-of-gold: material of
coloured silk and gold thread.

cloud: 3.2.51–2: (a) sad look; (b)
ominous sign.

clouts: 4.7.6: (a) cloths: bandages;
(b) thumps.

clown: rural fellow.

colour: 1.3.32: pretext.

comes: 1.4.44: becomes.

common body: ordinary populace.

comparisons: gay comparisons:
(per.: a) showy insults; (b) fine
advantages.

competitor: partner.

compliment: ceremony.

compose: come to an agreement.

composition: pact, agreement.

composure: character, disposition.

conclusion: (i: 4.15.28:)
judgement; (ii: 5.2.351:) test.

condition: disposition, character.

conference: conversation.

confound: (i: 1.1.45; 1.4.28:)
waste; (ii: 2.5.92; 3.2.58:)
destroy.

confusion: ruin, destruction.

considerate: reflective.

consideration: reflection.

contestation: conflict.

continent: container.

contrive: plot.

conversation: behaviour.

convey: transfer.

corrigible: submissive.

count (n.): mark, score-tally.

countenance: out of
countenance: into shame.

course (vb.): 3.13.11: pursue.

courtier: wooer.

court of guard: guard-room.

crack: detonation (e.g. of thunder).

crescent: growing.

crownet: coronet.

cup (vb.): 2.7.113, 114: ply with
drink.

curious: inquisitive.

curstness grow: rancour add.

cut (n.): 1.2.162: (a) wound; (b) slash in a garment; (c) vulva.

cut (vb.): 3.7.22: cross.

Cydnus: river of Cilicia (later Turkey).

dæmon: guardian spirit.

daff: doff.

dame: lady.

dare (n.): defiance.

darkling: in darkness.

darting: javelin-hurling.

dear: 2.5.105: (a) costly; (b) dire.

declined: (i: 3.11.47:) drooping; (ii: 3.13.27: a) in misfortune; (b) grown old.

defeat: (i: 4.14.69:) vanquish; (ii: 5.1.65:) thwart.

defend: forbid.

deign: accept.

demuring: looking gravely.

demurely: 4.9.31: (a) gravely; (b) prematurely.

denounce: declare war.

dependency: submission.

deputation: **in deputation**: as my envoy.

derogately: disparagingly.

determine: (i: 3.13.161:) dissolve; (ii: 4.3.2:) conclude; (iii: 4.4.37:) decide; (iv: 5.1.59:) arrange; **determined**: 3.6.84: ordained.

devise: feign, invent.

Dido and Æneas: legendary lovers.

digest: arrange.

diminutive: dwarf.

disaster (vb.): 2.7.15: (a) blight, mar; (b) deprive of stars.

discandy: melt, liquefy.

discontent (n.): malcontent.

disguise (n.): 2.7.120: (a) foolery; (b) intoxication.

dislimn: 4.14.10: (a) dissolve, (b) vanish.

dismission: order to depart.

dispatch (vb.): finish quickly.

disponge: discharge.

dispose: come to terms, settle matters.

dissuade: 4.6.13: persuade.

distract: 3.7.43: divide, disrupt.

distraction: (i: 3.7.76:) dispersal; (ii: 4.1.9:) fury.

dodge (vb.): prevaricate.

doom: judgement.

Doomsday: the final day, when God judges everyone.

dotage: infatuation.

drave: drove

dress (vb.): 5.2.271: (a) clothe; (b) prepare.

drink . . . vapour: inhale . . . odour.

droven: driven.

dumb (vb.): render inaudible.

duty: reverence, respect.

ear (vb.): plough.

Eastern Star: Venus, the morning star.

easy to't: easy to reach it.

effects: realisation.

Egypt: (i: 1.1.29, etc.:) the land of Egypt; (ii: 1.3.41, etc.:) Egypt's Queen.

embattle: form the battle-line.

embossed: frenzied.

emphasis: intense expression.

employ: send with a commission.

enforce: (i: 1.3.7; 5.2.124:) compel; (ii: 2.2.104:) emphasise.

enfranchèd: liberated.

enter: 4.14.113: (a) enrol; (b) introduce well.

entertain: (i: 2.1.47:) receive;
(ii: 2.7.60:) consider.

entertainment: (i: 3.13.140:)
reception; (ii: 4.6.17:)
employment.

envy: malice.

epicure: 2.7.49: (a) glutton;
(b) atheist.

estate: situation.

estridge: goshawk.

eternal: famed for ever.

exeunt: they go out.

exigent: final crisis.

exit: he or she goes out.

expedience: hasty departure.

extemporally: by improvisation.

extend: seize on.

eye (n.): 3.9.2: sight; **i'th'eyes**: in
her sight.

eye (vb.): 1.3.97: seem.

eyne: eyes.

factor: agent.

fairer: 1.2.15–17: (a) more noble;
(b) more beautiful; (c) with
lighter skin.

fairy: 4.8.12: enchantress (*O.E.D.*).

fall (vb.): 3.7.39: befall; **fall
upon**: intrude on.

falliable: 5.2.255: (error for)
infallible.

false-played: treacherously
gambled.

fame: (i: 2.6.64:) glory; (ii:
3.13.119: a) report; (b) rumour.

farthest: utmost.

fast and loose: a cheating game.

fat (n.): vat.

fate: (i: 3.13.169:) good fortune;
(ii: 4.8.34; 4.14.135:) destiny.

favour: (i: 2.5.38:) face; (ii:
3.13.134:) lenience.

fear (vb.): 2.6.24: frighten.

feature: appearance.

feeder: parasite.

fetch in: surround.

fever (vb.): induce tremors in.

file: rank (of soldiers).

find: 1.2.27: find by palmistry.

finis: the end.

firm: 1.5.44: constant.

flag: **vagabond flag**: drifting
reed.

flaw: crack.

fleet (vb.): sail.

fleeting: inconstant.

flourish (n.): fanfare.

flush: lusty.

fly off: break away.

foil: 1.4.24: (a) fault; (b) disgrace.

foison: abundance.

fool: 1.1.13; 5.2.302: (a) play-
thing; (b) dupe.

for: 4.12.37: instead of.

forbear: (i: 1.2.117; 2.7.37:) leave
alone; (ii: 1.3.11; 1.3.73;
2.7.94:) stop this; (ii: 5.2.174:)
withdraw.

formal: 2.5.41: (a) sane; (b) normal.

forspeak: argue against.

Fortune: goddess of chance.

foul: (i: 1.2.67; 4.9.19:) ugly;
(ii: 2.7.96; 4.6.38:) dirty.

frame (vb.): (i: 2.2.216:) perform;
(ii: 5.1.55:) conform.

fretted: 4.12.8: (a) chequered;
(b) eroded.

front (n.): face.

front (vb.): confront.

frustrate: baffle, defeat.

fugitive: deserter, runaway.

fully: (i: 1.1.50:) to the utmost;
(ii: 4.9.33:) completely.

Fulvia: Antony's first wife.

furious: desperate.

Fury: snake-haired avenger.

garboil: brawl.

gaudy: festive.

general tongue: widespread report.

gest: exploit.

give off: 4.3.22: end.

go: 1.2.59: (a) walk; (b) become pregnant; (c) copulate; **go off**: 4.13.6: depart; **go to**: 3.3.2: (a) don't be silly; (b) that's enough.

goal: **goal for goal of**: even with.

Gorgon: petrifying snake-haired female.

got upon: won from.

grace (n.): (i: 2.2.135:) merit; (ii: 2..2.153; 5.2.28:) favour; (iii: 3.12.19; 5.2.24:) generosity; (iv: 4.2.38:) blessings; (v: 5.2.344:) gracious charms.

grace (vb.): 4.14.136: (a) honour; (b) adorn.

graceful: 2.2.65: favourable.

gracious: 2.5.86: agreeable.

grate (vb.): annoy.

grave: 4.12.25: deadly.

green sickness: anaemia of young females.

greet: 2.1.40: (a) meet; (b) fraternise; (c, as 'gree') agree.

grew: 5.2.88: produced crops.

grief: 2.2.105: grievance.

gypsy: (i: 1.1.10: a) vagabond gypsy; (b) Egyptian; (c) low woman; (ii: 4.12.28:) vagabond gypsy.

Hail, Cæsar: 3.6.39: (a) Health to Cæsar; (b) We salute Cæsar.

halt (vb.): 4.7.16: limp.

hand: **unto thy hand**: in readiness.

haply: perhaps.

happiness: good fortune.

harness: armour.

haunt (n.): 4.14.55: (a) resort; (b) abode of ghosts.

hautboys: oboes.

head: 4.1.10: chief officer.

hearted: brave.

hearts: brave followers.

hearty: 4.2.38: (a) brave; (b) loving.

heaviness: sorrow.

heavy: (i: 3.7.39:) cumbrous; (ii: 4.15.32:) heavily; (iii: 4.15.40:) sad.

Hector: Trojan hero.

helm: (i: 2.1.33:) helmet; (ii: 2.2.213: a) wheel; (b) tiller.

Hercúlean: like the powerful Hercules.

hie thee again: hurry back

high-battled: in command of great armies.

hint: opportunity.

holding (n.): chorus of a song.

homager: vassal.

home: 1.2.101: plainly.

honest: 1.5.17: chaste.

honesty: (i: 2.2.97; 3.13.41:) integrity; (ii: 5.2.251: a) truthfulness; (b) chastity.

Hoo! (cry of elation): Oh yes!

hope (vb.): 2.1.39: suppose, expect.

huswife (pron. 'huzzif'): 4.15.44: (a) hussy; (b) housewife; (c) whore.

idleness: (i: 1.2.126; 1.4.76:) failure to act; (ii: 1.3.92–3: a) folly; (b) frivolity; 1.3.94: (a) so-called sloth; (b) pain.

ignorance: 3.10.7: stupidity.

immoment: unimportant.

immortal: 5.2.245–6: (error for) mortal.

imperious: imperial.

import (vb.): concern, involve.

impress (n.): conscription.

inclination: disposition.

in: you'll be in: 2.7.30: you'll be intoxicated.

inclip: embrace.

ingross: gather indiscriminately.

injurious: hostile.

intend: 2.2.45: mean.

intent: meaning.

intrinsicate: 5.2.301: (a) intricate; (b) hidden.

iron: 4.4.3: armour.

Isis: Egyptian goddess of fertility, the moon and the earth.

issue: outcome.

it own: 2.7.40, 44: its own.

Jack: coarse male.

jaded (vb.): driven like decrepit horses.

jealousy: suspicion.

joint (vb.): unite.

Jove: Jupiter, supreme god.

jump (n.): venture.

Juno: goddess, consort of Jupiter.

Jupiter: supreme Roman god.

kind (n.): his kind: what is natural for him.

kite: bird of prey.

knave: (i: 1.2.67; 1,4,21; 2.5.102:) low fellow, wretch; (ii: 4.14.12, 14; 5.2.3:) servant.

known: 2.6.83: met.

lady trifles: ladies' trivia.

land service: 2.6.94: (a) thieving; (b) military service.

languish (n.): lingering disease.

lank (vb.): grow thin.

large: 3.6.93: free, unrestrained.

lated: benighted.

launch: lance.

law (interj.): 4.4.8: indeed.

laying: 2.2.60: imputing.

lead: full of lead: weighed down by grief.

leaner: less important.

length: 4.14.47: endurance.

Lethe: underworld river; its waters induce amnesia.

Letheed: oblivious (as if he had drunk of Lethe).

levelled at: 5.2.332: (a) aimed at; (b) guessed.

Lichas: servant of Hercules.

lictor: beadle.

lief: gladly.

lie . . . upon thy hand: remain unsold.

lieutenancy: dealt on lieutenancy: acted by proxy.

light: 2.2.184: bright.

lightness: levity.

liver: (supposedly) seat of passions such as love.

loathness: reluctance.

loofed (vb.): 3.10.18: departed.

Lo thee!: Look, done!

lottery: 2.2.248: (a) allocation; (b) prize.

lowering: 1.2.121: declining.

lowness: abject state.

luxuriously: lecherously.

made more: 2.6.114: counted for more.

main: 1.2.186: supreme.

make price: haggle.

mallard: wild drake.

mandragora: soporific mandrake-juice.

Mars: god of war.

master-leaver: runaway servant.

matter: less matter: less substantial news.

mean (n.): 3.2.32; 4.6.35: means.

measure: (i: 1.1.2:) limit; (ii: 2.6.37:) quantity; (iii: 3.4.8:) allocation; all measures: the gamut of fortune.

mechanic: menial.

med'cine: 1.5.37: (a) doctor; (per. b) gold-making elixir.

meetly: fairly good.

member: 1.2.161: (a) person; (b) limb; (c) penis.

memory: 3.13.163: offspring.

Mercury: herald of the gods.

meréd question: specific basis of the quarrel.

merely: utterly.

merit: desert.

methinks: I think.

mettle: 1.2.138: 'spunk': (a) courage; (b) sexual vitality.

mince (vb.): make light of.

minister: servant.

minute: **by the minute**: incessantly.

mirth: joke.

Misena: Misenum: naval base in Italy.

missive: messenger.

misthink: misjudge.

mock: 5.1.2: render ridiculous.

modern: familiar.

modesty: moderation.

moe: more in number.

moiety: half.

monstrous: unnatural.

monument: massive tomb.

moody: melancholy.

moon: 3.12.6: month.

mortal: deadly; **mortal house**: body.

motion: (i: 1.4.47; 3.3.19:) movement; (ii: 2.3.13:) inner self.

motive: cause.

Mount Misena: promontory on the Bay of Naples.

muleters: muleteers: mule-drivers.

muss: game in which small items are scrambled for.

mutiny: quarrel.

mutual: well-matched.

name: **have a name**: be nominally; **have no names**: be illegitimate..

Narcissus: a beautiful youth.

nature: (i: 1.2.8; 5.2.97, 99:) creative Nature; (ii: 1.2.91:) character; (iii: 2.2.206; 2.2.223:) natural realm; (i: 5.1.29:) natural feeling; (ii: 5.2.291:) life; **sides of nature**: body.

naught: (i: 3.10.1:) ruined, lost; (ii: 3.5.21; 4.15.78:) worthless.

Neptune: the sea-god.

Nereides: sea-nymphs, daughters of Nereus.

nerve: muscle.

Nessus: centaur who killed Hercules.

nice: 3.13.180: easy-going.

nick (vb.): cut short.

Nilus: the river Nile.

nod (vb.): 3.6.66: beckon with a nod.

nonpareil: unrivalled.

nothing of: 2.2.85: irrelevant to.

number (vb.): versify.

observance: perception.

occasion: (i: 1.2.133:) exigency; (ii: 2.6.125:) opportunity.

odds: (i: 2.3.27, 38:) balance of advantage; (ii: 4.15.66:) distinction of worth.

o'ercount: (i: 2.6.26:) outnumber; (ii: 2.6.27:) cheat.

office: duty.

opinion: self-esteem.

oppression: foe's power.

orb: (i: 3.13.146:) sphere; (ii: 5.2.85:) globe.

ordinary (n.): public meal.

orient (adj.): splendid.

Out . . . !: 1.2.37: Wrong . . . !

over-plus: in addition.

owe: 4.8.31: own.

pace: 2.2.69: cause to proceed steadily.

pack cards: arrange cards to cheat.

pageant: show.

paint: use cosmetics.

palate (vb.): 5.2.7: enjoy taste of.

pale (vb.): 2.7.65: enclose.

palled: waned.

palter: haggle.

pants: on the pants triúmphing: triumphantly on the panting breast.

paragon (vb.): compare as an equal.

parcel (n.): product.

parcel (vb.): 5.2.162: (a) augment; (b) calculate.

part (n.): (i: 1.3.36:) personal feature; (ii: 3.2.32; 3.4.14:) side.

part (vb.): (i: e.g. 1.2.174:) depart; (ii: e.g. 1.3.87:) separate.

particular (n.): personal concern.

partisan: halberd: long-shafted weapon.

pass: 3.2.27: testify.

patch up: make from scraps.

pause (n.): hesitation.

pelleted: of ice-pellets.

Peloponessus: southern peninsula of Greece.

pendent: overhanging.

penetrative: piercing.

period: end, termination.

Philippan: used at the battle of Philippi.

Phœbus: 1.5.29; 5.2.314: (a) Phœbus Apollo, the sun-god; (b) the sun; Phœbus' car: Apollo's chariot.

piece (n.): (i: 1.2.149:) specimen; (ii: 3.2.28:) paragon; (iii: 5.2.99:) masterpiece;

bruisèd pieces: battered pieces of armour.

piece (vb.): augment.

pinch (vb.): 2.7.5: annoy.

pinion (n.): outer wing-feather.

pinion (vb.): clip a wing to prevent flight.

pink: 2.7.110: (a) reddened; (b) half-closed; (c) squinting.

place: lower place: subordinate.

placed: 5.2.237: fixed.

plainness: plain speaking.

plate (n.): silver coin.

plate (vb.): clothe in armour.

pleached: folded.

plucked: denuded.

plumpy: plump.

pocket up: put away: disregard.

point (n.): tagged lace fastener.

pole: 4.15.65: (a) standard; (b) Pole Star; (c) maypole.

Pomepy: great Pompey: 1.5.32: Sextus Pompeius.

port: (i: 4.4.23:) city gate; (ii: 4.14.53:) bearing, deportment.

possess: 2.7.97: dominate;

possess . . . of: 3.11.21: give.

post (n.): courier.

power: (i: 3.7.57, 76:) army; (ii: 3.12.36:) bodily faculty.

practise on: plot against.

pray in aid: beg the help.

precedence: preamble.

pregnant: obvious.

prescript: written orders.

present: 2.2.143: sudden; from the present: irrelevant.

presently: promptly, immediately.

president: supreme ruler.

price: make price: haggle.

prithee: please; **I prithee**: I beg you.

process: summons, command.

project (vb.): present.

prompt: 3.13.75: inclined.

proof: 4.8.15: a strong layer.

propertied: endowed.

property: quality.

prorogue: defer.

prosecution: pursuit.

proud: 2.5.69: great.

prove: 1.2.31: experience.

puppet: actor in pantomime (*O.E.D.*).

purchase: acquire.

purge: (i: 1.3.53:) seek purgation; (ii: 4.14.124:) get rid of.

purse up: pocket.

puzzle: 3.7.10: (a) distract; (b) perplex.

quail (vb.): intimidate.

quality: nature, character.

quarter (n.): sufficient time and/or space.

quarter (vb.): carve up.

queasy: disgusted.

question (n.): subject of quarrel.

quick: (i: 1.2.106:) intelligent; (ii: 5.2.215:) quick-witted.

quicken: (i: 1.3.69:) give life to; (ii: 4.15.39:) revive.

quit: (i: 3.13.65:) leave; (ii: 3.13.124:) reward; (iii: 3.13.151: a) repay; (b) punish.

race: (i: 1.3.37: a) trace; (b) sign; (c) offspring; (ii: 3.13.107:) lineage.

rack: drifting cloud.

range (n.): line of battle.

ranged: extensive.

rank of gross diet: stinking of coarse food.

rarely: exceptionally.

rashness: thoughtlessness.

rate (vb.): (i: 1.4.31:) scold; (ii: 3.6.25:) allocate; (iii: 3.11.69:) be worth.

raught: caught.

rebound: 5.2.104: (a) impact; (b) influence.

record: history.

reels (n.): 2.7.90: (a) revels; (b) staggering.

regiment: authority.

register: record, chronicle.

rend: divide.

render: give up.

renege: renounce.

report (n.): 2.2.52: reporter.

reputation: honour.

require: (i: 1.2.190; 5.1.63:) need; (ii: 3.12.12, 28; 3.13.66:) request.

revolt (n.): desertion.

revolt (vb.): desert.

revolution: cycle of time.

rheum: 3.2.57: (a) catarrh; (b) watery eyes.

ribaudred: (per.) debauched.

riggish: randy, lustful.

right: 4.12.28: typical.

rightly: truly.

riotous: raving.

rivality: equal partnership.

rive: rend, tear.

rule: **by the rule**: properly.

rush (n.): reed.

sad: 1.3.3: (a) serious; (b) sad.

safe (vb.): (i: 1.3.55:) ensure; (ii: 4.6.26:) provide safe-conduct for.

safe (adj.): 4.15.26: secured from humiliation.

said: **well said**: well done.

sails: (i: 2.2.198; 3.10.15; 4.12.4:) sails; (ii: 2.6.24; 3.7.49; 3.11.55:) ships.

salt: (i: 2.1.21:) salacious, randy;
(ii: 2.5.17:) preserved in salt.

saucy: (i: 3.13.98; 4.14.25:)
insolent; (ii: 5.2.213: a)
insolent; (b) lascivious.

savage: savage cause: reason to
be ferocious.

scald: 5.2.214: (a) foul;
(b) coarse.

schoolmaster: private tutor.

scotch: gash.

scrupulous faction: strife over
details.

seal (vb.): conclude matters.

seel: sew shut.

self: 5.1.21: same.

semblable: similar.

sennet: trumpet-call.

sets down: is encamped.

several: separate.

shadow: delusive image.

shake off: reject.

shard: 3.2.20: (a) dung-lump;
(b) scaly wing.

sheets (vb.): covers like a sheet.

shiny: bright.

shrewd: severe.

shroud: shelter.

sickly (adv.): with distaste.

Sicyon: Greek town near Gulf of
Corinth.

sides of nature: body.

sign (vb.): bode, augur.

sir: 4.15.85: serving companion;
Sir: 5.2.119: lord.

sirrah: 5.2.228: you servant.

slippery: fickle.

smock: petticoat.

snaffle: bridle-bit to restrain a
horse.

so: (i: 2.5.94:) even though;
(ii: 3.2.20; 3.13.52; 4.4.28:)
good, very well.

sober: coolly sensible; soberly:
with dignity.

soft: 2.2.88: gently.

solemnity: ceremonial event.

sottish: stupid.

sour: embittered.

sovereign: potent.

spaniel (vb.): follow fawningly.

speak with: 2.6.25: fight.

spleet: 2.7.120: (a) slur;
(b) confuse.

spoil: despoil.

spoke: 2.2.170: fought.

spot: (i: 1.4.12:) star; (ii: 4.12.35:)
blemish.

sprightly: (i: 4.7.15:) cheerful; (ii:
4.14.53: a) lively; (b) spectral.

spurn: kick.

squadron: body of troops.

square (n.): 3.11.40: (a) troops in
square array; (b) squadron;
kept my square: been
virtuous.

square (vb.): quarrel.

square (adj.): fair, true.

stablishment: confirmed
possession.

stain: 3.4.27: eclipse.

stale (n.): urine.

stall (vb.): dwell.

stand: 3.2.49: remain motionless;
stands up for: claims to be.

state: (i: 1.2.87:) situation;
(ii: 2.2.44:) imperial power.

station: immobility.

staunch: hold us staunch:
(a) bind us together; (b)
preserve our mutual loyalty.

stay . . . by: 2.2.182: cope.

still (adj.): (i: 1.2.106; 4.11.1:)
inactive; (ii: 2.6.118:) quiet;
(iii: 4.15.28:) silent.

still (adv.): constantly.

stomach (n.): inclination.

stomach (vb.): resent.

stomaching: resentment.

stretch: extend.

strike: (i: 2.7.93:) broach;
(ii: 5.2.357:) afflict.

stroyed: destroyed.

strumpet: whore.

studied: thought out.

study on: ponder.

success: 3.5.6: outcome.

sue: petition.

sum: gist.

surfeit: nausea.

swerving: transgression.

swoond: swoon, faint.

synod: assembly of the gods.

tabourine: portable drum.

tackle (n.): rigging.

take: 4.2.37: overcome; 'Take
all!': 'Let the winner take all!';
take in: conquer.

tall: 2.6.7: brave, bold.

targe: light shield.

target: light shield.

tart (adj.): sour.

Telamon: (here) Ajax, the crazed
warrior.

temper (n.): moderation.

temperance: (i: 3.13.121:) chastity;
(ii: 5.2.48:) moderation.

tempt: 1.3.11: test.

tend: 2.2.212; 4.2.24, 32: wait
on.

terrene: terrestrial.

thereabouts: thinking that.

Thetis: a sea-goddess.

thick: (i: 1.5.65:) repeatedly; (ii:
5.2.210:) foul; (iii: 5.2.296:)
dense.

thicken: 2.3.27: darken.

think: 3.13.1: brood, reflect
sadly.

thought: 4.6.35, 36: melancholy.

three-nooked: tripartite.

throw upon: bestow upon.

Tiber: river of Rome.

tight: deft, skilled.

time: 1.3.42; 3.6.82: situation
now.

timelier: earlier.

tinct: 1.5.38: (a) alchemist's
elixir; (b) colour.

tissue: 2.2.204: twisted thread.

toil: net, snare

tokened: spot-marked.

tongue: general tongue: widespread report.

touch (n.): pang.

touch (vb.): (i: 2.2.145; 5.1.33:)
affect; (ii: 3.12.31:) sully, taint;
(iii: 5.2.327:) meet.

tóward: 2.6.73: impending.

toy: trivial item.

traduce: censure.

treaties: 3.11.62: proposals to be
agreed.

treble-sinewed: triply muscular.

trencher: wooden dish.

trespass (n.): offence.

tribunal: raised platform.

trick: (i: 4.2.14:) freakish action;
(ii: 5.2.75:) habit.

trifle: lady trifles: women's
trivia.

trim (n.): trappings, armour.

triple: 1.1.12: one of three;
triple-turned: thrice unfaithful.

triumph: 4.14.20: (a) Roman
triumph; (b) trump-card.

triumphant: 2.2.190: splendid.

Triumvirate: Trio of Rulers.

true: 2.6.97–8: (a) honest;
(b) sincere; (c) natural.

trull: whore.

try: 2.7.122: test.

undo: (i: 2.2.210; 3.4.17:) annul, cancel; (ii: 2.5.106; 5.2.44:) ruin, destroy.

unequal: unjust.

unexecuted: unused.

unfold with: exposed by.

unpolicied: his plot thwarted.

unqualitied: demoralised.

unseminared: castrated.

unstate: set aside.

up: 3.5.11: shut up, confined.

urge: 2.2.51: cite as motive.

use (n.): **in use**: in trust.

use (vb.): (i: 2.6.128:) exercise; (ii: 3.7.65:) be accustomed.

vacancy: 1.4.26: (a) leisure; (b) empty hours.

vant: van: front.

vantage: prospects of victory.

varletry: mob, rabble.

varying: full of changes.

vent (n.): discharge.

Vesper: Venus as dusk-goddess.

vessels: **strike the vessels**: (a) open the casks; (b) beat the goblets.

vestal: virginal priestess of Vesta.

vial: small bottle.

viands: food.

vilde: 4.14.22: vile.

vouchsafe: condescend.

wage (vb.): contend in rivalry.

wail: bewail, lament.

waned: 2.1.21: (a) withered; (b) 'wanned': pallid.

wassail (n.): carousal.

waste (n.): lavish consumption.

waste (vb.): consume.

watchman: sentry.

weet: know.

well said: 4.4.28: well done.

wharf: river-bank.

what: 5.2.310: why.

wheels: **go on wheels**: run smoothly.

whole: 3.7.71, 74; 3.8.3: (a) undivided; (b) healthy, unimpaired.

wild: (i: 1.2.46; 2.7.120:) licentious; (ii: 5.2.311:) savage, stormy.

will: 3.13.3: sexual desire.

window (n.): eyelid.

window (vb.): place in a window.

witch: **the witch take me**: may I be bewitched.

withal: with.

woot: wilt, wilt thou, will you.

word (n.): 1.2.131; 2.2.49; 3.1.32: watchword, motto.

word (vb.): ply with empty words.

work: **has work**: struggles.

worky-day: commonplace.

worm: snake.

worship: 4.14.87: revered merit.

yare (adj.): nimble, quick; **yare** (adv.): quickly; **yarely**: nimbly.

yield: (i: 2.5.28:) depict; (ii: 4.2.33:) reward.